School Leadership in a Diverse Society

Helping Schools Prepare
All Students for Success

School Leadership in a Diverse Society

Helping Schools Prepare All Students for Success

Carlos R. McCray
Fordham University

Floyd D. Beachum
Lehigh University

INFORMATION AGE PUBLISHING, INC.
Charlotte, NC • www.infoagepub.com

Library of Congress Cataloging-in-Publication Data

A CIP record for this book is available from the Library of Congress
http://www.loc.gov

ISBN: 978-1-62396-529-7 (Paperback)
       978-1-62396-530-3 (Hardcover)
       978-1-62396-531-0 (ebook)

Printed in the United States of America

In Loving Memory of

Wilma Williams
Mary Sailes
Josephine Lowery
Constance Oates

Contents

Foreword

Ira Bogotch
Florida Atlantic University

A mbitious. Transformative. Controversial. I use these words to describe the twists, turns, and detours that characterize the intellectual journey that Carlos McCray and Floyd Beachum present in *School Leadership in a Diverse Society: Helping Schools Prepare All Students for Success*. Their objectives, however, are quite straightforward. They are seeking to build a solid bridge between multicultural education and school leadership theories and practices.

Historically, the two fields—multiculturalism and school leadership—have developed separate and apart with minimal crossover analyses. Whereas the former has been viewed as relevant primarily with respect to classroom pedagogies and curricular debates, school leadership has taken a managerial turn away from curriculum and instruction. McCray and Beachum recognize that the next phase of scholarship is for a more thorough or ambitious integration. For educational leadership, bridge building (see Chapter 4 in this volume) has only recently become a necessary aspect of development (see Boske, 2012; Tooms & Boske, 2010). Thus, what we have here is a richer and deeper discourse of schooling because of this integration. And this could not come at a more important time in our history as accountability in the form of test scores has made separate and apart dis-

School Leadership in a Diverse Society, pages xi–xiii
Copyright © 2014 by Information Age Publishing
All rights of reproduction in any form reserved.

courses the ways in which we categorize schools and students. That has to be contested, as McCray and Beachum ably demonstrate. In short, the field of educational leadership needs to move past its managerial constraints in order to embrace broad and deep meanings of diversity in education and society. Educational leadership itself has to become transformative (Shields, 2012).

Conversely, McCray and Beachum call for an expansion of multicultural ideas and practices to include school leadership, as policies and practices. Given the long-standing and entrenched positions taken by some ethnic studies researchers (vis-à-vis multiculturalism), some readers may find this book controversial. I see it, however, as offering a mutually beneficial relationship whereby multicultural theorists (as well as curriculum theorists) engage with leadership ideas/practices in order to be more successful in bringing about whole school and social reforms. This is the focus of *School Leadership in a Diverse Society.* As systematic analysts, McCray and Beachum acknowledge the progression of social justice ideals by tracing the history of segregation, desegregation, post-Brown reforms, and the emergence in the late '60s and '70s of diverse and separate ethnic studies (as in Black Studies, Chicano Studies, Puerto Rican Studies, Indigenous Studies, etc.). But what McCray and Beachum see as educationally sound is a fundamental return to the principles of multiculturalism as a way to bring us together educationally as a nation while still addressing the urgent urban problems of African Americans and other marginalized peoples of color in city schools. This argument sets McCray and Beachum apart from other powerful and progressive voices in critical education. It also demonstrates the authors' passion for justice and rage in the face of injustices.

Each section of the book includes distinct genres: theory, application to practice, and case studies. This organization allows readers to follow either the logic of the book or to choose a new logic. I don't think McCray and Beachum will mind how readers engage with the ideas in this book. The point is to make this book work for all of us! Our shared goals as educators are to make a material difference in the lives of children and their families, and to do so, we have to be innovative and ambitious, not just compliant and hopeful. McCray and Beachum invite you to think along with them and join the conversations for school-community development. On every single page, you cannot help being aware of the struggles and the high stakes faced by everyone involved today in the fight to save public education.

The field of educational leadership, particularly school leadership, is slowly maturing beyond a series of "to-do" lists, whether based on common-sense axioms or administrative know-how. One way to view this book is as an interruption of the *status quo* in which today's school reform initiatives come from business leaders who advise federal and state government officials. Oppositionally, McCray and Beachum demonstrate why educators, not external authorities, should be driving school and community reforms. What this means is that it is the responsibility of school leaders (here I include educational leadership researchers as well as practitioners) to offer counterhegemonic discourses and methods (see Schoorman & Bogotch, 2010) that depict education and schools as primarily for promoting economic advancements such that the idea of public education is as a common good (Hostetler, 2005). Diversity and multiculturalism, McCray and Beachum remind us, are ways to reconnect with efforts to develop local school communities, collectively.

By acknowledging this local, national, and global fact, it should be obvious that no "one best systems' thinking" ought to trump local community initiatives. It should also be obvious that the need-to-know hierarchical structures of bureaucratic schools/systems are relics from a failed past. How should we know this? If school leadership and diversity were integrated, there would be more evidence of equitable and social justice realities in and out of schools. Two quotes from this text illustrate the significance of their ideas:

> Our notion of success consists of students being exposed to a holistic educational experience, which entails students' educative process going beyond literacy and numeracy.... A *pedagogy of self-development* calls on educators to deliver a holistic educational experience to students of color, where there is specifically a cultivation of their sense of *self-realization* and *self-assertion*. (p. 4)

> Alas, we are not convinced that the sole focus on literacy and numeracy along with shutting and reopening schools is in and of itself a remedy for academic success among African American students and students of color. (p. 20)

As professors and researchers, McCray and Beachum translate school-community from frustrations to hopes into lived realities. This book takes us beyond teaching methods, beyond traditional leadership as management, and beyond standardized testing as the primary purposes of public education. The United States may be on an exceedingly long "middle passage" from Goals 2000-ISSLC-NCLB-Race-To-The-Top-Common Core—top-down reforms all. Today's reforms are historical accidents (Bogotch, 2011) that have taken public education away from its mission to bring social mobility to an experimental society. Let's join with McCray and Beachum in struggling against accidents, missteps, and especially injustices. Ambitious. Transformative. Controversial. Enjoy.

Preface

School Leadership in a Diverse Society: Helping Schools Prepare All Students for Success is the culmination of several years of interest and research on issues regarding diversity and leadership in U.S. K–12 schools. Its origins began years ago when we were doctoral students at Bowling Green State University. We both had an interest in issues regarding diversity and the desire to infuse this interest with educational leadership. What followed would be a growing research agenda on our part with regard to multicultural education and leadership, the achievement gap, urban school leadership, cultural collision (Beachum & McCray, 2011), and culturally relevant pedagogy (Ladson-Billings, 1995). Our work was also informed by the work of Dr. Taylor Cox (1994, 2001), who examined issues of diversity and change in organizations. Professor Cox made careful and critical connections between the success of diversity initiatives and the role and responsibility of leadership. As we searched the literature from the late 1990s into the turn of the 21st century, we noted plentiful references to diversity with regard to curriculum and pedagogy, but little information regarding diversity and school leadership. In recent years, more literature has emerged that connects the dots of diversity, community, social contexts, and leadership. It is within the context of this work that we offer *School Leadership in a Diverse Society: Helping Schools Prepare All Students for Success* as a resource for practitioners who are dealing with increasing diversity and its ensuing issues, and for scholars who seek research or data that informs educational leadership on issues of multiculturalism and diversity. This book outlines some of our

School Leadership in a Diverse Society, pages xv–xxiv
Copyright © 2014 by Information Age Publishing

work on educational leadership and proposes new trajectories as we look toward the future.

The purpose of this work is to broaden the scholarly dialogue in educational leadership and to address the changing role of the American school principal in the 21st century with regard to increasing diversity in the United States. This book seeks to provide empirical, theoretical, and practical insight into the role of school principals dealing with an ever-increasing multicultural student population. We will cover an array of issues we believe are critical in order for the 21st century school principal to be effective and relevant. A primary inquiry that needs to be made is: Are school leaders taking seriously the increasing social and cultural diversity in their schools? It is the school principal who sets the tone for the school culture and who provides the vision as to the direction of the organization (McCray, Alston, & Beachum, 2006). We endeavor to help scholars and practitioners have a better understanding of the importance of the diversity of their students and to give them the tools to appropriately lead schools in ways that ensure all students, regardless of their life circumstances and status, are provided a school climate that promotes high academic achievement and a sense of belonging.

Multiculturalism and diversity preparation are needed in our society today; in fact, more so now than when schools first started to make an earnest effort to integrate in the 1970s (Nieto & Bode, 2008). Just as it seemed the United States was making significant progress dealing with injustice issues that have plagued the country for hundreds of years, a recent plethora of issues has arisen to remind us that multiculturalism and diversity preparation is still vitally necessary to help fight intolerance and prejudice within our schools. This moment in the American educational experience is rife with complexities and ironies.

The state of American education today is one that has resulted from our collective past, policies, and decisions. Seldom are the solutions to educational problems simple, and too many times there are various complexities that characterize different sides of educational issues. K–12 schooling's trajectory is one of progression and regression, gains and losses, tremendous strides and difficult lapses. Much of this is centered on issues of diversity. For instance, even though the 21st century is full of promise and potential for K–12 students, many school districts are more segregated today than in the past. While many people are familiar with *Brown v. Board of Education* (1954) and how it struck down "separate but equal" and sanctioned integrated schools, few are familiar with the school bussing cases that followed and the slow march back to segregation. In *Milliken v. Bradley* (1974), the use of bussing students of color to surrounding suburban districts was severely limited. According to Tatum (2007), "In this case, the Court prohibited court ordered bussing across district lines unless there was proof that the actions of the school districts had created the racial disparities between them" (p. 8). The problem here was not any malicious intent on the part of school districts to segregate students, but rather it was the historical residential housing patterns that were deeply connected to public schools. Thus, as more people of color migrated to cities on the East Coast and Midwest (Wilkerson, 2010), White flight to the suburbs was triggered.

Public schools are largely funded by local property taxes (and in some cases by sales taxes and/or state funding). Thus, in cases in which you have an economically stable community, they can generate more money for their local schools than struggling or impoverished communities can. Unfortunately, when residents who have higher incomes move, as in the case of *White flight* or *Black trek*, they leave behind an economically vulnerable neighborhood that could easily slide into decline (Beachum & McCray, 2011; Dyson, 2004; McCray, 2008). Wilson (2009) agreed,

> With the departure of higher income families, the least upwardly mobile individuals in society—mainly low-income people of color—are left behind in neighborhoods with high concentrations of poverty and deteriorating physical conditions. . . . Typically, these communities also suffer from substandard schools, many with run-down physical plants. (p. 42)

In another case, *Board of Education of Oklahoma City v. Dowell* (1991), the Court ultimately endorsed neighborhood school policies in which students were to attend the schools in and around their neighborhood. Tatum (2007) indicated that this decision "had the ripple effect of federal judges releasing other schools from their court-ordered desegregation plans" (p. 10). Therefore, one case essentially crystallized White flight from inner-city areas to the suburbs, while the next case sanctioned neighborhood schools. Together, these two cases formed firm pillars of policy-related segregation that is more *de facto* (of the fact) than *de jure* (of the law). This situation severely undermines the intention of integrated schools, where a diverse mix of students would interact, learn with and from each other, and foster generations of collaboration and better cross-racial understanding. Tatum (2007) gravely warned,

> As school districts move back to neighborhood school policies, the next generation of White students will likely have less contact with people of color than their predecessors did. Particularly for young White children, interaction with people of color is likely to be a virtual reality rather than an actual one, with media images (often negative ones) most clearly shaping their attitudes and perceived knowledge of communities of color. The progress that

has been made in the reduction of racial prejudice that can be associated with shared school experiences is at risk of stalling. (p. 14)

In addition to the legal and historical challenges to diversity in schools, there is the issue of educational emphasis. Since around 1957 with the launch of Sputnik, the United States has been on a long journey toward educational excellence and school reform (Cuban, 2004). This notion of excellence has been characterized by increased offerings in math and science, higher standards for K–12 schools, increased accountability for teachers and administrators, and increased student achievement as usually evidenced by standardized test scores. Newspaper stories and national reports, such as *A Nation at Risk* (1983), helped to push public attitudes toward this definition of educational excellence.

> *A Nation at Risk* made many allegations of numerous "failures" of U.S. schools and went on to charge that the educational achievement of U.S. students was dismal in comparison with that of students of other lands. Further, it described U.S. schools as being not very well organized and run and depicted educators in them as being a dispirited and not very able lot. (Owens, 2001, p. 10)

A Nation at Risk emerged as the first major report disseminated by the Department of Education, which had only recently been created (Hewitt, 2008). The report solidified the agenda of educational excellence by way of requiring more accountability and higher standards, and helped to open the door for measuring student achievement by standardized test scores.

In 1989, several national education summits took place, which included state governors, CEOs, and even President Bill Clinton; and in 1994, *Goals 2000* was enacted. More formally known as the *Goals 2000: Educate America Act*, it provided a plan for higher educational standards, increased measurement and tracking of student achievement, and support for schools as they work toward meeting these goals (Cunningham & Cordeiro, 2003). The act proposed that significant educational milestones be achieved by the year 2000, such as increased graduation rates, increased math and science achievement, comprehensive adult literacy and citizenship, and an end to violence and drugs in American schools. Although this legislation ultimately failed, it provided the roadmap for the reauthorized *Elementary and Secondary Education Act* (ESEA) in 2001, also known as *No Child Left Behind* (NCLB). This legislation fossilized the educational excellence agenda. NCLB would represent federal education legislation that significantly impacted all U.S. schools. It enforced a rigorous system of standards, instituted high-stakes testing (and public reporting), clearly defined adequate yearly progress (AYP) for all schools, and outlined a system of rewards and sanctions for *not* meeting AYP.

Beachum, McCray, and Huang (2010) opined, "Educational excellence is now defined by high stakes testing, greater accountability, school choice, and achieving an adequate yearly progress" (p. 53). To be clear, we should strive for educational excellence in U.S. schools. The problem occurs when the policies and practices do not necessarily produce the intended outcomes and when other educational values are sacrificed in the name of excellence. Obiakor and Beachum (2005) wrote, "In its most noble sense, excellence is an ideal that should permeate American educational ideology, but its usage has veered from more principled conceptions and has been used to compete and conflict with equity" (p. 7). Similar to our journey toward educational excellence, we have also struggled with a quest for educational equity.

Educational equity has more to do with every student receiving what they need in order to be successful. This concept impacts not only resources received but also the motivation and attention of students. Equality supports the idea that all students deserve to receive the same. The problem is that "remedies based on equality assume that citizens have the same opportunities and experiences" (DeCuir & Dixson, 2004, p. 29). Obiakor and Beachum (2005) elaborated, "The lack of access to opportunities and qualitatively different life experiences are many times linked to issues of race/ethnicity, gender, and social class" (p. 5). This situation creates a tension in education between endeavors toward equity, such as *Brown v. Board of Education*, and equality-based initiatives centered on excellence, like *No Child Left Behind*. Examples of educational equity are evidenced in the historic *Brown v. Board of Education* decision (1954) and even in 1965 when President Johnson signaled affirmative action efforts with the signing of Executive Order 11246 (Cox, 1994; Tatum, 2007). The United States would bear witness to several efforts to integrate K–12 schools through bussing, quotas, and even armed intervention from the National Guard, which represented concrete moves in the direction of educational equity for all students. President Lyndon Johnson increased the federal government's role in education with his "War on Poverty," which created programs like Head Start. Policies like this exemplified the national mood toward equity-based programming in general and also within education specifically.

The 1970s witnessed more change with the emergence of the Individuals with Disabilities Education Act (IDEA) (Tosh & Edwards, 2009). IDEA guaranteed an appropriate public school education to all students and specifically addressed children with disabilities. As time progressed, new concepts and pedagogical approaches informed the educational equity effort. James Banks advocated for a diversity-based reform movement called multicultural education, which would place the experiences of students of color along side that of White students and give voice to the histories, cultures, and worldviews of these students (Banks & Banks, 1989; Banks, 1991). Scholars like Festus E. Obiakor bridged multicultural education and special education and gave critical insight into misidentification, misassessment, miscategorization, misplacement, and misinstruction (Obiakor, 2011).

Later, Gloria Ladson-Billings pushed our pedagogical understandings with a framework called culturally relevant pedagogy. Irvine (2010) stated that culturally relevant pedagogy "builds on the premise that learning may differ across cultures and teachers can enhance students' success by acquiring knowledge of their cultural backgrounds and translating this knowledge into instructional practice" (p. 58). Similarly, Howard (2003) commented on culturally relevant pedagogy by noting,

> In order to provide more meaningful knowledge and skills for teaching in today's cultural context, teacher educators must be able to help preservice teachers critically analyze important issues such as race, ethnicity, and culture, and recognize how these important concepts shape the learning experience for many students. More specifically, teachers must be able to construct pedagogical practices that have relevance and meaning to students' social and cultural realities. (p. 195)

Both of these statements capture the essence of culturally relevant pedagogy. More recently, equity-based solutions in education have been focusing on the concept of social justice. Although originally undertheorized and underexplored in education (Gewirtz, 1998), social justice is now becoming a recognized part of the discourse in education. Social justice, with its contested meanings and definition (Shoho, Merchant, & Lugg, 2005), tends to focus on anti-oppression and marginalization (Radd, 2008; Theoharis, 2009), social power (Bogotch, Beachum, Blount, Brooks, & English, 2008), a moral and ethical inclination (Dantley, Beachum, & McCray, 2008), and advocacy as well as reflection (Bogotch, 2002). Thus, it has been a long hard road toward educational equity, with a great distance that still needs to be traveled.

The key to the success of many modern organizations is leadership; our schools are no different. The leadership qualities, knowledge, and skills needed today are different from previous years. Fullan (2004) agreed, "The more complex society becomes and the more we experience rapid, unpredictable, nonlinear change in our organizations and our world, the more sophisticated leadership must become" (p. xiii). Today's successful school

leaders understand the value of collaboration, team building, and empowerment. For leaders themselves, this requires some key characteristics. Over
the course of more than 25 years of research on leadership, Kouzes and
Posner (2007) have identified four major characteristics: *honesty, forward-
looking (visionary), inspiring, and competent.*

Honesty

Honesty in leadership brings to mind words like values, integrity, character, and morals. This is important because we want a sense of authentic-
ity in our leaders. "If we follow someone who's universally viewed as having an impeccable character and strong integrity, then we're likely to be
viewed the same" (Kouzes & Posner, 2007, p. 33). With regard to diversity,
honesty is a very relevant quality. Leaders must be honest with themselves
and others when dealing with tough issues. Honesty forces school leaders to look inward to examine what they really believe about their leadership abilities, their teachers, and their expectations for students. Dantley
(2010) called this critical self-reflection, which is a process whereby "the
educational leader [comes] to grips with his or her sacred, genuine, or
unvarnished self" (p. 216).

Forward-Looking (Visionary)

It is difficult to talk about true leadership without discussing vision.
Most people want leaders who are forward-looking and have a plan for taking their organization to a better place. Simply put, vision is "the ability
to imagine or discover a desirable destination toward which the company,
agency, congregation, or community should head" (Kouzes & Posner, 2007,
p. 33). It identifies where the organization should go and outlines a strategy
for getting there. Of course, followers are essential in this situation because,
as Fullan (2004) stated, "To realize the vision there must be people below building capacity and shared commitment so that the moral imperative becomes a collective endeavor" (p. 161). As we think about leadership
for diversity, vision is an especially crucial component. Forward-thinking
leaders engage others in the vision by expressing personal passion for the
effort, providing a compelling rationale for diversity, and communicating
effectively to people at all levels of the organization (Cox, 2001). In schools,
this usually means formulating policies and practices around the unyielding belief that all students can learn and that they will receive what they
need to be successful.

Inspiring

A common hallmark of leadership is inspiration. "A leader must be able to communicate the vision in ways that encourage people to sign on for the duration and excite them about the cause" (Kouzes & Posner, 2007, p. 34). Additionally, leaders must have energy and enthusiasm (Fullan, 2004). If people do not see the vision come to life in the words and actions of their leader, they may not entirely commit their full efforts, talents, and skills. "Effective leaders make people feel that even the most difficult problems can be tackled productively" (Fullan, 2004, p. 6). Inspiration is a key attribute as school leaders deal with diversity-related issues. Issues such as cultural mismatch, cultural collision (Beachum & McCray, 2011), increasing urban school dropout rates, overly aggressive discipline, overrepresentation of Black students in special education, underrepresentation of girls in math and science, and underteaching of students of color are all difficult diversity-related problems that administrators must grapple with in their schools. As they engage in this struggle, they must also bring their staff and communities along, providing clarity, optimism, and hope. The leadership necessary involves inspiration that is undergirded by conviction (Walters, 1987).

Competent

Leadership is much more than a position of authority. "Leadership competence refers to the leader's track record and ability to get things done" (Kouzes & Posner, 2007, p. 35). Leaders must have a certain amount of content knowledge, educational background, and relevant experience, as well as sound judgment. Thus, leaders should have the appropriate skill-set relevant for their work and the knowledge to make appropriate decisions. Competence is of particular importance with regard to diversity. Leaders who move ahead too quickly without enough knowledge about their student body are simply asking for trouble. Therefore, educational leaders must inform themselves with regard to issues of multiculturalism and diversity specific to their particular school and community setting (Beachum & Obiakor, 2005), and embrace the values they promote (McCray & Beachum, 2010). Part of the aforementioned honesty quality is really believing in what you promote as a leader. Simply put, people want to be sure you know what you are talking about, believe in what you espouse, and can facilitate action on the subject.

Leadership challenges related to issues of diversity are not going away. And they cannot be avoided. Schools, and school leaders especially, will have to find ways to address these challenges (Dantley et al., 2008; Obiakor, 2001; McCray, Wright, & Beachum, 2007; Terrell & Lindsey, 2009). This will require a restructuring of "antiquated leadership models and frameworks" (Beachum & Obiakor, 2005, p. 85). Cunningham and Cordeiro (2003) stated that "new frames can accentuate previously unnoticed possibilities" (p. 24). Our hope is that this book will provide new frames that draw much-needed attention to contemporary diversity-related issues in school leadership.

In sum, this discussion has highlighted three themes. First, the segregation/resegregation discussion represents how our contemporary educational context was and is shaped by past legal decisions, showing how history and context continue to impact our educational system today. Second, the excellence/equity debate illuminates the fact that our educational policies and practices are supported by our flawed educational philosophies. Third, the leadership discussion reminds us of the importance and influence of school leaders. Furthermore, the same general leadership qualities found in contemporary organizational leadership literature blend seamlessly into leadership for diversity and success for all students in an educational context. This book is written in a way that addresses these areas. Law, history, philosophy, and worldviews all impact leadership; and leadership impacts the ultimate success or failure of a school.

This book contains three specific sections. The first section consists of theoretical chapters examining current and relevant issues dealing with diversity and multicultural constructs, in which school leaders should be firmly grounded. The second section of the book ` includes chapters devoted to the type of leadership needed to initiate, implement, and sustain multicultural education within the school. And finally, the third section of the book explores new horizons for multicultural education, with specific concentration on the emerging concept of culturally relevant leadership. The chapter following each section (i.e., chapters 3, 5, and 7) consists of a case dealing with the theories, issues, and research that have been discussed in the preceding chapters of that section.

In La Fontaine's fable, the hare is quick, clever, high on hubris, and a loser. The tortoise is slow and purposeful; it adapts to the terrain and is a winner (Fullan, 2004, p. 185).

This simple but enlightening fable reminds us that the quick and easy answer is not always the right one. School leadership today, though fast-paced, is highly complex. It requires purposeful inquiry, astute perception, and informed decision-making—slow-knowing with purpose, not swift action with hubris. Ironically, we are not talking about taking forever to see changes or achieve results. What we are encouraging is a process of leadership that engages rather than ignores diversity, recognizes history and context, embeds significant knowledge in leaders so they may act with confidence, and promotes the facilitation of new ideas or frameworks in practice. "A long series of small efforts despite its slow pace, often turns out to be the quickest way to make the organization—and the world—a better place" (Badaracco, 2002, p. 2). We can only hope that this book will have a global impact; but more realistically, we simply hope that it can make your school a better place.

—**Carlos R. McCray**

Floyd D. Beachum

Acknowledgements

This book has been one the most challenging endeavors I have taken on in recent memory. For some strange reason, I thought this book would be just as easy to write as our first co-authored book, *Cultural Collision and Collusion: Reflections on Hip-Hop Culture, Values, and Schools.* I was wrong! It has taken us over 2 years to complete the book from start to finish. And I am very grateful to all my family, friends, and colleagues who kept the faith in me in ensuring that this book was completed.

First, I would like to acknowledge my mother and father, Willie and Joyce McCray, whose unyielding support made this endeavor possible. I will always cherish their love for as long as I live. Mom and Dad, thank you for all you have done. I would also like to thank individuals from my community where I grew up in Alabama. The old axiom, it takes a village, is true. There have been many individuals from my community who have had a great impact on me throughout the years. So I would like to give a shout out to all of those individuals and especially Dr. James Wright, retired Associate Dean at Auburn University in Montgomery, Alabama. Dr. Wright has been an excellent mentor and friend throughout the years. Professor Wright, thank you very much for all your support. You are a scholar, educator, mentor, but more importantly a true friend.

I would also like to thank other friends and family members who have reached out to me with their kind words urging me to keep plugging away. I would like to thank LTC Cecil Copeland III; Marion Smith, Jr.; Derrick Bryant; Kelvin Wright; and Maj. Jibraun A. Emerson for their constant belief in

School Leadership in a Diverse Society, pages xxv–xxviii
Copyright © 2014 by Information Age Publishing
All rights of reproduction in any form reserved.

me and making those crucial phone calls to inquire about my work. Thank you for your support.

Throughout an endeavor such as this one, we need those in our corner who can inspire and are willing to be advocates for our work. Thus, I would like to thank the book series editor, Dr. Jeffery Brooks, for his unequivocal belief in our ability to finish this book. I am eternally grateful to you for those constant emails you sent reminding us of the importance of our scholarship. Jeff, you have been a great colleague throughout the years, but more importantly, a true friend. Thank you for your unwavering support in this journey! In addition to thanking Jeff, I would also like to thank all of my colleagues at Fordham University who have been so gracious and supportive of me.

Finally, I would like to dedicate this book to my little cousins, Fayth Bryant, Caitlyn Copeland, Alana Melton, Corinne Barnett, and Isaiah White. I hope they look upon this work as they get older and find inspiration in achieving their goals in life. I am thoroughly convinced that the next family generation is in good hands!

Carlos R. McCray
New York, New York

The desire to write a book is a noble goal that inspires many. The reality of completing that book can be another story. On this project we have found that dedication, tenacity, compromise, focus, and commitment all were needed. At the same time, the constant support from friends and family helped to sustain us. Therefore, I would like to first thank my supportive wife, Katerri Stacks-Beachum, who dealt with my long nights of writing and trips out of town to make sure that this book came into existence. I would also like to thank my son, Devin, who just gave a smile, kiss, hug, or laugh and really kept me grounded. The both of you mean so much to me, and I love you both very much.

I would also like to thank my mother, Mattie Suggs-Beachum, who always asked how the book was coming along and how I was doing. Sometimes it is just nice to know that someone cares about your well-being—thanks Mom! Thank you to my extended family in Saginaw, Michigan, the Quad-Cities (Florence, Muscle Shoals, Sheffield, and Tuscumbia) there in northwest Alabama, and all of our relatives in the Chicago, Illinois, area.

On this journey I have met some great people in many different places. Thanks to everyone who contributed to my undergraduate experience at Alabama State University. Special thanks to Drs. Dorothy Autrey-Harris and

Allan Stewart, who were both instrumental in my development. Thank you to all of my friends and former students from Selma High School, where I first began teaching. An extra special thanks to my doctoral program in Educational Administration and Leadership Studies at Bowling Green State University. Dr. Eugene Sanders was a large part of my recruitment and introduction to higher education. Later, Dr. Patrick Pauken would serve as my dissertation chair. Thanks to the both of you and the faculty. My first tenure-track position was at the University of Wisconsin-Milwaukee. I would like to thank Dr. Gail Schneider and my other colleagues from UWM. It was there I really learned about urban education and higher education.

I would also like to thank my colleagues at Lehigh University, especially in the College of Education. Thank you to Dean Gary Sasso and Chair George DuPaul for their leadership. In the area of educational leadership, I would like to thank Dr. George White, who is a constant source of support, information, and big ideas. Special thanks to the other educational leadership faculty, Perry Zirkel, Jill Sperandio, and Roland (Ron) Yoshida, Jon Drescher, and Louise Donohue. And thanks for the support of all other faculty in the College of Education. In the College of Education, I would also like to thank Mary Yotter (Coordinator for Educational Leadership and Counseling Psychology), Donna Ball (Academic Coordinator), and Adafo L. Austin (doctoral student).

I have had the incredible opportunity to learn from some great mentors. These include Drs. Na'im Akbar, Michael E. Dantley, Linda Tillman, Ira Bogotch, Fenwick English, and James E. Davis. A special thanks to Dr. Festus E. Obiakor, who took personal interest in my development as a scholar and person. His mentorship has been priceless over the years. At the same time, I have now had the opportunity to mentor and/or meet some great up-and-coming scholars like Terrence Green (doctoral student), Drs. Darius Prier, Emery Petchauer, Decoteau J. Irby, Christopher Yawn, and Ty-Ron Douglass. I would also like to thank Stan Brewer, my former student from Selma High School, who is not in the academy, but has turned out to be a great young man—stay focused and keep up the good work.

I would also like to thank some graduate students who helped on this project. Thank you to Frederick Brandon LaRue, Terrina Price, and Anne Marie Fitzgerald.

Finally, I would like to thank a man who has provided clear vision, sound direction, and steadfast stewardship. Extra special thanks to Mr. Peter Bennett for his gracious support for urban education and Lehigh University.

Floyd D. Beachum
Bethlehem, Pennsylvania

Carlos and Floyd would also like to thank the following:

Organizations:

AERA (American Educational Research Association)
http://www.aera.net/default.aspx

UCEA (University Council for Educational Administration)
http://www.ucea.org/

Barbara L. Jackson Scholars Program
http://www.ucea.org/jackson-scholar/

Colleagues and Friends:

Jeffrey Brooks, Ira Bogotch, Michael Dantley, Linda Tillman, Bruce Cooper, Greg Goodman, Sheldon Marcus, Gerald Cattaro, Beatrice Samson, Kathleen M. Cashin, Toby Tetenbaum, Dean James Hennessy, Dean Peter Vaughan, Michelle D. Young, Khaula Murtadha, Maria Gonzales, Catherine Marshall, Kathleen Brown, Gary Crow, Catherine Lugg, James Koschoreck, James Scheurich, Mark Gooden, Gerardo Lopez, Mariela Rodriguez, Judy Alston, Lisa Bass, Terry Orr, George Theoharis, Christa Boske, Joanne Marshall, Michael Jennings, Audrey Dentith, Betty Merchant, Sonya Douglass Horsford, Alan Shoho, Cindy Reed, Anthony Normore, Gaetane Jean-Marie, James V. Wright, Hayward Richardson, Marc Lamont Hill, James Peterson, Gloria Rodriguez, Chance Lewis, Jerlando Jackson, James Moore, Lamont Flowers, Rich Milner, Cosette Grant-Overton, Juan Gilbert, Marvin Lynn, Rene Antrop-Gonzalez, Thankdeka Chapman, Raji Swaminathan, Edgar Epps, Marty Sapp, Brenda Townsend, Gwendolyn Webb-Johnson, Monika Shealey, Wanda Blanchett, Beverly Cross, Martin Scanlan, Anthony "Tony" Frontier, Clarence Thomas, and Lisa Chavers.

SECTION I

1

Utilizing Multicultural Education for a Pedagogy of Self-Development

The first decade of the 21st century has not produced the educational results that policymakers, educators, and parents would have hoped for concerning the education of culturally and linguistically diverse (CLD) learners, particularly African American students (McCray, 2008, Noguera, 2008). The current results in education for students of color have proven demoralizing. The prognosis over the past few years has been that the concentrated educational efforts (i.e., Goals 2000 and No Child Left Behind [NCLB]) by policymakers would lead to a decrease in the academic achievement gap among CLD learners and their White counterparts. It was also thought that such polices would reduce the number of students dropping out of school and increase the graduation rate of students of color.

Unfortunately, the latest national educational reports have indicated that in numerous categories, many African American students and other CLD learners are falling further behind. This is especially true for African American males. In 2010, the Council of the Great City Schools issued a

School Leadership in a Diverse Society, pages 3–21
Copyright © 2014 by Information Age Publishing
All rights of reproduction in any form reserved.

report titled, "A Call for Change: The Social and Educational Factors Contributing to the Outcomes of Black Males in Urban Schools." This report dealt with the educational experiences of African American students. The report concluded that African American students, males in particular, are still lagging behind their White, Asian, and Latino counterparts. African American students seem to have higher rates of school suspensions as well as lower graduation rates. The report also found that African American students had lower overall academic achievement than their White counterparts. With regard to school suspension, a form of punishment that schools heavily rely on for discipline (New York Times, 2010a, p. A19), the Council of the Great City Schools' report concluded that Black students were more likely than all other students to receive excessive suspensions and expulsions from school.

These statistics are disturbing for a number of reasons. First, African American students, especially African American boys, over the years have been suspended more than any other group (McCray & Beachum, 2006). Second, research has been clear regarding the correlation between students who are expelled on a regular basis and those who end up forfeiting their education (Beachum & McCray, 2011). In December of 2010, the *New York Times* reported that the Baltimore school system, a district that is 88% Black, handed out 26,000 school suspensions in the year 2004. Not only are African American students ushered out of school on a routine basis, but in many instances, they are disenfranchised academically by a rigid and militaristic school climate.

This 2010 report issued by the Council of the Great City Schools shows that there is still a tremendous amount of work to be done if we are to ensure that all students achieve academically. We realize that in the age of accountability and assessment, the success of students, specifically CLD learners, is narrowly defined (Ravitch, 2010). When we speak of students' academic success, we proffer that success is more than being conditioned or prepared to pass a standardized test or to perfect rote memorization only to not recall such information a few months later. Here, our notion of success consists of students being exposed to a holistic educational experience, which entails students' educative process going beyond literacy and numeracy. Ravitch (2010) stated it succinctly in her best seller, *The Death and Life of the Great American School System: How Testing and Choice are Undermining Education,* when she opined that a holistic education involves students being exposed to a comprehensive curriculum involving history, language arts, and social studies as well as politics. She also indicated how crucial it is for students to learn how to think, communicate, and respectfully listen to the opinions of others. Unfortunately, in today's political climate, all anyone has to do is pay close attention to our political process to realize how judicious her statement is on what constitutes a cogent education for all students.

This pronouncement by one of the most respected educational historians in the country is what we feel undergirds the concept of a pedagogy of self-development (McCray & Beachum, 2011b; McCray, Grant, & Beachum, 2010). A *pedagogy of self-development* calls on educators to deliver a holistic educational experience to CLD learners for the cultivation of their sense of *self-realization* and *self-assertion*. And we believe that multicultural education is an appropriate curriculum to help ameliorate the aforementioned conditions of African American students and other CLD learners, as well as to enhance their sense of self-development.

It is negligent and irresponsible for educators and scholars to stand idly by and watch as the most vulnerable of students are further hindered by the political posturing, scapegoating, and constant bombardment of pseudochange by policymakers and nefarious outside entities. Instead, school leaders and educators must muster their moral purpose and courage to meet their responsibilities head-on to ensure that all students are prepared to meet the challenges of the 21st century and fortified with the appropriate skillsets.

Keeping a Competitive Edge

The United States' global competitive edge is at stake in ensuring that all students are educated. Unfortunately, it is becoming increasingly transparent that the United States is falling further behind other nations in reading, mathematics, and science, according to the Organisation for Economic Co-operation and Development and its Programme for International Student Assessment (PISA). This report concluded that among industrialized nations, the United States is somewhere around the middle of the pack in reading test scores and more toward the back in science and math. In fact, the PISA findings showed that the United States was dead last, tied with Ireland, in the math portion of the test (New York Times, 2010b, p. A22). President Obama echoed these test results when he spoke to a college audience in North Carolina. The President indicated that "Fifty years later, our generation's Sputnik [the Soviet Union's launching of its famous spacecraft] moment is back, . . . [India and China are] suddenly plugged into the world economy. As it stands right now, America is in danger of falling behind" (New York Times, 2010b, p. A22).

Despite evidence by PISA and other researchers who have studied the global academic achievement gap and have concluded that even when comparing high achieving students in the United States with their overseas counterparts, the United States still lags behind (Wagner, 2008). The prevailing viewpoint among some educators is that such scores are a result of the United States' heterogeneous population that other nations do not have. When educators make this argument, it is generally a veiled way of indicating that other nations do not have to put up with all the *stuff* we have to put up with in the classrooms. In other words, other countries do not have to teach the Black and brown kids, or the kids with limited English proficiency. This argument amounts to nothing more than excuses that capitulate to the notion that Black and brown students are not capable of learning at very high levels. It is in essence an acquiescence to the *deficit theory*—the notion that diverse student learners are inherently suspect due to their cultural and social background and are therefore not capable of high academic achievement (Solorzano, 1997).

The corollary of such views by our educators is summed up in a report edited by Samuel Halperin and his colleagues (2008) titled, "The Forgotten Half Revisited: American Youth and Young Families, 1988–2008." The report concluded that students who had not acquired a college education or specific job training find it increasingly difficult to secure full-time employment. Of course, the corollary of not having adequate education and full-time employment is higher unemployment, lower rates of homeownership, higher incarceration rates, and higher incidences of teen pregnancies and crime (Wilson, 2009). "The Forgotten Half Revisited" report (2008) is also clear in its elucidation that full-time employment for young people of color was 20% to 30% lower than their White counterparts. Nevertheless, such an appalling statistic regarding the disparate rates of employment for Whites and people of color should not come as a surprise to anyone.

Also, in a subsequent report on the academic achievement of Black males, the findings were once again demoralizing. The report, ironically titled, "Yes We Can: The Schott 50 State Report on Public Education and Black Males" (Schott Foundation for Public Education, 2010), stated that nationwide, only 47% of Black males graduate from high school. According to the findings, "The rate at which Black males are being pushed out of school and into the pipeline to prison far exceeds the rate at which they are graduating and reaching higher levels of academic achievement" (Schott Foundation for Public Education, 2010, p. 1). The report concluded that a "deliberate, intense focus is needed to disrupt and redirect the current educational trajectory of Black males" (Schott Foundation for Public Education, 2010, p. 1).

These statistics concerning African American students, especially Black males, are deeply disturbing. To address this dire situation, educators and school leaders must find the courage and vision to deal with such issues. We believe what is missing from the educational experiences of many students is a sense of purpose. Many students, especially students of color, feel as if schools have not made an adequate attempt to accommodate who they are and what they inevitably bring to school with them. And yes, we would tend to agree with students in this regard. In many instances, schools have inadvertently or maybe purposefully (Beachum & McCray, 2011) stifled what Paulo Freire (1998) called the ingenious curiosity of students. And we believe that a pedagogy of self-development for students of color, undergirded by the principles of multicultural education, is appropriate to cultivate CLD learners ingenious curiosity while enhancing their academic achievement.

A pedagogy of self-development entails fostering *self-realization* and *self-assertion* in CLD learners. Thus, in order for this to take place, educators and school leaders must have an understanding of the specific forms of capital that students of color have at their disposal. Yosso (2005) has found that students of color have at least six forms of capital that educators and school leaders often fail to recognize or understand: *familial, resistant, linguistic, aspirational, social*, and *navigational*.

We believe multicultural education is a proven and valued concept that enhances alternative forms of capital in students of color, thereby cultivating in them a *sense of self-realization* and *self-assertion*. Multicultural education has a long history of helping African American students and other CLD learners find solace within oftentimes hostile educational terrains. Nevertheless, some scholars claim that multicultural education is somewhat antiquated and that academics should focus their energy on more updated theories and methods. Needless to say, we do not believe this to be the case. McCray (2010) wrote the following concerning the continuing need to embrace the principles of multicultural education:

> The United States is seeing exponential changes in its demographic make-up with regard to increases in its population of people of color. . . . Thus, school principals [and educators] must have a central role in initiating and infusing multicultural concepts and ideas into their school's culture. . . . In the era of constant change where change is championed by political parties, businesses, and of course schools; educational scholars and practitioners might have been too quick to jump off the multicultural initiative for more catchy terminology. (p. 38)

The Origins of Multiculturalism

The notion of developing a curriculum to enhance the educative experience of all students regardless of their race or gender originated from the

"African American scholarship and ethnic studies movement" (J. A. Banks, 1996, p. 39), which coincided with the Civil Rights Movement in the 1960s (J. A. Banks, 2001). Some of the earliest and most significant contributors of multicultural education were individuals such as Gwendolyn Baker, James A. Banks, Geneva Gay, and Carl A. Grant; and many of these scholars' early works consisted of research scholarship geared toward African American Studies (J. A. Banks, 1996). Some of Banks' earliest works involved a concentration on African American history due to the influence of African American historians, such as the venerable John Hope Franklin and Benjamin Quarles.

Prior to multicultural education officially arriving on the scene, there were several scholars, practitioners, and educators advocating for diverse perspectives within the school and classroom (Brown, 2005; McCray et al., 2007; Ortiz, 1982; Russo, 2004; Tillman, 2003). And before full-scale integration of public schools took place in the United States, many of the nation's civil rights and professional organizations (i.e., American Council on Education, National Council for Social Studies, and the National Conference of Christian and Jews) had begun to examine schools across the United States to determine the best way to fight racism as well as classism (J. A. Banks, 1995). This momentum, which became known as the intergroup education movement, took place in the 1940s and 1950s. "The intergroup education movement . . . responded to the race riots and violent conflicts that occurred in the nation's cities in the early 1940s" (J. A. Banks, 1995, p. 37). One of the basic premises of this movement was to place pressure on colleges of education to implement programs that helped teachers in training to become better prepared to educate African American students, as well as other students of color (J. A. Banks, 1995).

Although the African American ethnic studies movement and the intergroup education movement had similar objectives and strategies concerning diversity and inclusion, these two movements were little intertwined. The proponents of each group had different overall goals, and they differed to a great extent in their ethnicity as well. The proponents of the intergroup education movement were mostly White and existed inside the walls of academia. These individuals were routinely labeled as "liberal Whites" (J. A. Banks, 1995, p. 37). On the other hand, the proponents of the African American ethnic studies movement were mostly Black scholars in the field of history and those who learned under well-respected Black historians.

As African American students began to integrate into formerly all-White public schools in the 1960s and 1970s, they sought a curriculum that was inclusive rather than exclusive (J. A. Banks, 2001). African Americans and other ethnic minorities wanted a curriculum that celebrated their histories more than the curriculum that was being presented at the time. This endeavor by African Americans became known as the era of ethnic studies, one of the first stages of multicultural education that was designed to make the school curriculum more inclusive of minority groups. Grant (1995) found that, "A curriculum that is multicultural . . . highlights the history and contribution of all Americans and is infused throughout the entire kindergarten through the twelfth-grade program" (p. 719). Curriculum inclusiveness and increasing numbers of minority faculty and staff were the focal points for advocates of multicultural education in this early stage (J. A. Banks, 2001).

Although the ethnic studies phase of multicultural education was an important chapter for ensuring that non–Anglo Americans learn about their culture and heritage, educators involved in this phase soon realized that more efforts were needed to restructure the schooling process to enable students of diverse backgrounds to learn at a high level (Ramirez & Castaneda, 1974). Consequently, the ethnic studies movement progressed into a "multiethnic education" movement in the 1970s. The purpose of this development was to restructure the school environment as a whole and not focus solely on the curriculum (J. A. Banks, 1996, p. 40). The multiethnic education phase was designed to reform all mechanisms of the school structure, such as the delivery of instruction, counseling techniques, teachers' dispositions toward students of diverse cultures, and school policies that indirectly harmed students of color, such as tracking, misdiagnosing and labeling, and biased disciplinary procedures (J. A. Banks, 1996).

The Women's Movement of the 1960s and 1970s also had a major impact on multicultural education (J. A. Banks, 2001). Women and other disenfranchised groups began to question their representation in the school curriculum. They became advocates for more visibility and recognition of their respective groups. J. A. Banks (2001) observed, "When feminists looked at educational institutions, they noted problems similar to those identified by ethnic groups of color" (p. 6). One of the major problems identified consisted of the lack of contributions by women in school textbooks. Consequently, the Women's Movement and the Civil Rights Movement paved the way for the curricula in public schools to be critiqued and improved as it related to women and people of color (J. A. Banks, 2001).

The next phase in the history of multicultural education developed as a result of the variety of courses, practices, and programs that evolved to meet the needs of an increasingly diverse student population (J. A. Banks, 2001). For example, people with disabilities have become one of the greatest and most triumphant advocates for "educational change and inclusion" (J. A. Banks, 1996, p. 40). To many, multicultural education is seen historically and at present as a program of study designed to reexamine how groups of color were portrayed in history and to teach more factual content as it relates to groups of color (Gay, 1995). Many multiculturalists (Gay, 1995; Nieto, 2000) today have reexamined the concept of multicultural education and view it in a totality perspective, as it relates to the entire school climate; this approach allows students to achieve to their fullest potential (McCray et al., 2006). However, because multicultural education has had political liabilities associated with its nascent stage, the task many multicultural theorists face is to transform these political liabilities into "scholarly strengths" (J. A. Banks, 1996, p. 6). The "negative" aspects of multicultural education (i.e., it is too divisive and takes away from crucial subject matter) have kept many school leaders and educators from embracing it fully (McCray, Wright, & Beachum, 2004).

One concern that some scholars, such as Dantley (2002), raised concerning multiculturalism is the premise that some multicultural theorists have begun to compromise the basic foundation of multicultural education in order to appease would-be detractors. Taylor (2000) came to a similar conclusion:

> Although grounded in an era of change and vision of equality, [multiculturalism] has seen its goals diluted. Its original activist agenda has been diminished as the political climate shifts toward "color blindness" and attempts at an inclusive curriculum are reduced to cultural tourism. Some adherents believe that for multiculturalism to reassert its relevancy, it must openly identify oppression and struggle against it more explicitly. (p. 540)

Despite some negative views toward multicultural education from both sides (i.e., progressives and conservatives), we make a critical attempt in this chapter to show that multicultural education continues to have strong/fundamental relevancy in the academic achievement of CLD learners. According to J. A. Banks (2001), contemporary multicultural education encompasses five dimensions: *content integration, knowledge construction, prejudice reduction, equity pedagogy,* and *empowering the school culture.* We strongly believe that each of Banks' dimensions can build upon the alternative forms of capital that students of color possess, and thereby enhance their sense of *self-realization* and *self-assertion,* the principles of what we call a *pedagogy of self-development.*

Multicultural Education and Alternative Capital

In order for educators and school leaders to begin to change the current narrative of academic underachievement among many African American students and students of color, they must begin to divest themselves of the precept that capital comes in only one form. Brazilian scholar Paulo Freire (1998) cautioned educators against quickly dismissing what he called *ingenious curiosity* among traditionally marginalized students (i.e., poor students and many students of color or CLD learners). Freire equated ingenious curiosity among students with the notion of *common sense.* In other words, ingenious curiosity is the knowledge, know-how, and disposition that many students bring with them from their homes and communities. It is a way of understanding and comprehending among students, especially CLD learners, who are oftentimes marginalized because of their backgrounds. Such a prevalent manner of understanding and comprehending among students demands the attention and respect of the serious educator. According to Freire,

> The teacher who does not respect the student's curiosity in its diverse aesthetic, linguistic, and syntactical expressions; who uses irony to put down legitimate questioning . . . ; who is not respectfully present in the educational experience of the student, transgresses fundamental ethical principles of the human condition. (p. 59)

Freire went on to offer that the ultimate goal for educators is to parlay the student's ingenious curiosity into an *epistemological curiosity,* an inquisitiveness undergirded by more traditional academic edicts designed to enhance skillsets for participation in a democratic society.

In order for an epistemological curiosity to come to fruition, educators must recognize that students of color and students from low socioeconomic communities come to school with alternative forms of capital, as well as a lot of *common sense.* The entire notion of respecting ingenious curiosity in students of color is practically tantamount to the concept of multicultural education. There is an axiom in many parts of the Black community proffering that some of the smartest "young brothers" move in and out of the penal system. If there is any truth to this, one might surmise that educators have failed to parlay the ingenious curiosity of these students into an epistemological one because the pipeline to prison starts with the jettisoning of students from the classroom (Beachum & McCray, 2011).

McCray et al. (2010) have asserted that most schools are not positioned to take advantage of the ingenious curiosity that many students bring to school because *capital pluralism* within their school has ceased to exist. Capital pluralism is undergirded by the notion of cultural pluralism, which is the foundation of multicultural education. As we indicated earlier, "many school [leaders] are not comfortable with the increasing amount of diversity that is taking place in their respective schools and, alas, do not see a bona fide need to engage in cultural pluralism" (McCray, 2010, p. 38). McCray went on to indicate that,

> Scholars of multiculturalism . . . must debunk such notions that cultural pluralism does not have a place in schools. If anything because of the aforementioned increasing amount of social and cultural diversity that is occurring in our society and schools, such leaders who do not see a need for cultural pluralism must begin to capitulate vis-à-vis overwhelming data concerning the changing face of the United States. (2010, p. 38)

Thus, "capital pluralism is present in schools when educators not only acknowledge the existence of a macrocosm of social and cultural capital, but they also concede to the idea that . . . [students of color] have their own form of capital" (McCray et al., 2010, p. 237). Once again, Yosso (2005) found that the alternative capital students of color bring to school manifests into six distinctly different forms of capital: familial capital, resistant capital, linguistic capital, aspirational capital, social capital, and navigational capital. It is by educational leaders recognizing these different forms of capital students bring to school that they begin the journey of subscribing to the notion of pedagogy of self-development for CLD learners.

Familial capital is one of the alternative forms of capital identified by Yosso (2005) that is prevalent among students of color. This form of capital that students of color have at their disposal highlights their commitment to their respective communities as well as their understanding of the importance of family. Thus, we believe that J. A. Banks' (2001) notion of content integration is a dimension of multicultural education that can enhance the sense of familial capital in CLD learners.

J. A. Banks' idea of content integration is the process that allows the teacher to use materials from different cultures to make lessons more meaningful. We believe one of the reasons familial capital is connected to content integration is that content integration allows students to bring their own perspectives and realities into the lesson. To revisit Freire's (1998) notions of ingenious curiosity and epistemological curiosity, we argue that ingenious curiosity is equivalent to familial capital. Students of color pull from their family and community traditions that are oftentimes undergirded by a deep sense of history. When this sense of history and tradition is neglected within the classroom, it is highly unlikely that any substantive content integration is taking place, with the corollary being a suppression of epistemological curiosity being cultivated.

When students of color recognize that the curriculum is not intended for them, a form of resistance can develop within their disposition. It is resistant capital that allows students of color to recognize the structural impediments to their success within the educational establishment. Resistant capital "refers to knowledge and…skills fostered through oppositional behavior that challenges inequality" (Yosso, 2005, p. 80). Students in the 21st century are considered much more inquisitive and enlightened than their counterparts were some 50 years ago (Nisbett, 2009). Such precocious dispositions are partly due to the ever-increasing amount of stimulus from students' respective cultures. For example, in many communities, students experience stimuli from video games, certain television programs, computer applications, and of course, conversation with other adults (i.e., parents). These experiences have in many instances led educators to assign an adult value (i.e., capable, responsible, mature) to such students' dispositions and adjust their delivery of instruction accordingly (Nisbett, 2009). But as it relates to students who reside in urban areas (i.e., CLD learners), who in their own right are inquisitive and enlightened by certain environmental stimuli, the "adultification" that is projected on them is seen as an extreme cultural deficit in need of drastic correction (Beachum & McCray, 2011; Ferguson, 2001).

In many instances, this form of adultification that is projected on students of color often leads to students employing a form of resistant capital, which unfortunately reinforces educators' stereotypes toward them. Thus, J. A. Banks' (2001) dimension of knowledge construction can help parlay resistant capital in students of color into a pedagogical strength. "Knowledge construction is the process that allows educators and administrators the opportunity to critique work on multiple cultures to determine if any type biases were associated in the construction of knowledge" (McCray, 2010, p. 39). To once again pull from Freire's (1998) concepts of ingenious curiosity and epistemological curiosity, CLD learners should have a role in helping to critique any biases in the school curriculum (i.e., knowledge construction). Such an endeavor would draw on their ingenious curiosity brought with them from their homes and communities, and transform it into epistemological curiosity in which resistant capital is utilized as a strength instead of a weakness.

Along with familial and resistant capital, Yosso (2005) also identified linguistic capital as an alternative form of capital that students of color bring with them from their communities. We suggest that these three forms of capital—familial, resistant, and linguistic—undergird the notion of *self-realization* among CLD learners. Linguistic capital is a form of capital that students of color have that allows them to speak in multiple dialects, lexicons, and languages. According to Yosso (2005),

> In addition, these children [students of color] have been engaged par-
> ticipants in a storytelling tradition, that includes listening to and recount-
> ing oral histories, parables, stories,...and proverbs....This repertoire of
> storytelling skills may include memorization, attention to detail, dramatic
> pauses, comedic timing, facial affect, vocal tone, and volume, rhythm and
> rhyme. (pp. 78–79)

But McCray et al. (2010) cautioned that such alternative capital, although ubiquitous among CLD students, can be viewed by educators as a
detriment in need of "fixing." McCray et al. opined,

> This type of capital [linguistic] can easily be transformed into increased
> academic achievement but can also be viewed as a deficit need[ing] to be
> corrected. It can also be used as a gatekeeper to other forms of capital and
> perhaps, as a barrier to other goals and aspirations. Such a notion was il-
> luminated when Senator Harry Reid spoke of then presidential candidate
> Obama as being an attractive candidate to voters because he was "light
> skinned and had no 'Negro dialect.'" The Negro dialect or Black English
> vernacular (Hymes, 1981; Ogbu, 1999; Ovando, 2001; Perry & Delpit, 1998)
> that Senator Reid was speaking of might be sufficient grounds to block a
> Black person's ascendency to the White House as far as voters are concerned.
> However, it is a mistake for educators and school leaders to juxtapose the
> Negro dialect or Black English with Standard English as a barometer for
> aptitude or academic achievement. (p. 238)

This example illustrates how imperative it is for educators and school leaders to find a way to respect the diverse forms of communication that students of color bring with them from their homes and communities, and
turn them into meaningful pedagogical experiences.

Thus, equity pedagogy, another dimension of multicultural education,
is a suitable approach to help change the linguistic capital of students of
color into an academic strength. The essence of equity pedagogy is "the
process that allows teachers to use different teaching methods and styles
that tend to correlate with students of diverse cultural and social groups"
(McCray, 2010, p. 39). When educators are dismissive of how CLD learners
communicate and interact—their linguistic capital that undergirds learning—it nullifies any notion of equity pedagogy in the classroom. McCray
(2010) opined, "If critical [equity] pedagogy is going to be a part of the
educational classroom, educators have to make an effort to validate and not
invalidate the experiences that students bring to the classroom from their
respective communities" (p. 39). Thus, when equity pedagogy is nonexis-
tent in the classroom, the linguistic capital of students of color is curtailed.

As stated earlier, familial, resistant, and linguistic capital are linked to what we have identified as *self-realization* of a pedagogy of self-development. In addition, J. A. Banks' (2001) content integration, knowledge construction, and equity pedagogy are critical dimensions in capitalizing on these alternative forms of capital CLD learners have at their disposal, all of which can lead to *self-realization* among students. Self-realization occurs when students begin to feel as if their dreams can become reality as a result of an awakening process vis-à-vis a better understanding about the world in which they belong.

Now that we have identified critical dimensions of multicultural education and alternative forms of capital that can enhance self-realization in CLD learners, we will turn our attention to the other principle that undergirds a pedagogy of self-development, the idea of *self-assertion* among CLD students. We believe the remaining three alternative forms of capital—aspirational, social, and navigational—identified by Yosso (2005) can enhance a sense of *self–assertion* in CLD learners. *Self-assertion* is the idea that students have embraced the self-realization awakening from a mental, social, and academic perspective and are ready to seize upon any opportunities (McCray & Beachum, 2011b).

It should be of no surprise to anyone that the notion of self-assertion is assisted tremendously by educators and school leaders whom students encounter daily; and the alternative forms of capital that students of color bring to school with them provide critical pathways for this assistance. Recognition of students' aspirational capital, social capital, and navigational capital can contribute greatly to teachers assisting CLD learners in their preparation for and seizing of opportunities.

Yosso's (2005) aspirational capital highlights in CLD learners a sense of meliorism, that is, a belief that a cogent effort put forth in school will result in academic achievement. According to McCray et al. (2010), "Although many African American students, especially those from urban areas, face daily despair within their communities and schools, they still maintain a sense of optimism and hope for a better tomorrow through the means of their education" (p. 238). Such aspirational capital is enhanced by J. A. Banks' (2001) notion of empowering the school culture. The idea of empowering the school culture entails school leaders and educators creating a school climate that instills in CLD learners a sense of acceptance and belonging. Far too often, CLD students do not achieve at high levels because of low academic expectation from their teachers, which in many instances leads to a sense of frustration. Paradoxically, these same students are often recognized by their peers for their athletic prowess as well as their sense of style.

Foster (2009) found that most African American students have aspirations to achieve in school and in life. But Noguera (2008) found that as many CLD learners journey through the educational process, they lose their aspirations to excel academically. Noguera indicated that this loss of interest in academic pursuits usually happens around the middle school grade level. Here, you find students, especially African American males, who no longer believe in the notion of educational empowerment and begin to acquiesce to the notion that education is more for the privileged classes. In order for this prevailing narrative to be debunked, educators must tap into their students' academic aspirational capital by cultivating a school climate that empowers them socially as well as academically.

Yosso's (2005) remaining forms of capital, which we believe help cultivate *self-assertion* in CLD learners, are social and navigational capital. First, navigational capital is a form of capital that enhances in students of color the "ability...to maneuver through institutions not created with communities of color in mind" (Yosso, p. 80). In many instances, schools are undergirded by racial- and class-based hostility, which makes it extremely difficult for many CLD learners to achieve at high levels (Tatum, 2007). Nevertheless, some scholars (Allen & Solorzano, 2001; Alva, 1991; Perry, Steele, & Hilliard, 2003) have found that CLD learners, despite racial- and class-based hostility, have continually found ways to circumvent the militaristic and unaccommodating school culture and achieve academically.

We should use caution, however, in assessing CLD learners' ability to navigate through a hostile school environment. Unfortunately, a large number of students of color decide to remove themselves from the educational process (i.e., drop out) or are ushered out via multiple school suspensions and expulsions. Hersey, Blanchard, and Johnson (1996) insightfully noted, "Resignation or apathy occurs after prolonged frustration, when people lose hope of accomplishing their goal(s) in a particular situation and withdraw from reality and the source of their frustration" (p. 31). In many of our urban and impoverished schools, this form of resignation among students of color has seemingly intensified. It is of little consequence the amount of navigational capital students of color have at their disposal if structural arrangements in the school create obstacles to their piloting of the educational topography.

Just as CLD learners use navigational capital to help them make their way through hostile terrain undergirded by racist and classist ideology, they also use their social capital as a form of support to excel academically as well as socially. The version of social capital students of color possess, which is parallel with the mainstream's concept of social capital, also emphasizes taking advantage of networking opportunities. As mentioned, both social and navigational capital are needed for the cultivation of *self-assertion* in CLD learners, but such capital is often diminished by a school culture and climate that is undergirded by a sense of prejudice toward the most vulnerable. Banks' notion of prejudice reduction, a final dimension of multicultural education, is required to ensure that the social and navigational capital that students of color bring is not diminished. J. A. Banks (2001) noted that prejudice reduction occurs when school leaders and teachers create a school culture and classroom climate to "help students [and educators] develop positive attitudes toward different racial, ethnic, and cultural groups" (p. 21). Once again, we emphasize that it is extremely difficult for students of color to utilize their navigational and social capital when their school climate is undergirded by hostile racial and ethnic attitudes geared toward them. Diminished effectiveness of students' navigational and social capital can negatively impact their sense of *self-assertion.*

Pedagogy of Self-Development

Throughout this chapter, we have tried to illustrate how Yosso's (2005) notion of alternative capital intersects with J. A. Banks' (2001) five dimensions of multicultural education, and how these concepts can be used to enhance self-realization and self-assertion (i.e., a pedagogy of self-development) in CLD learners. Below (Figure 1.1), we have included a pedagogy of self-development diagram to help you visually comprehend our framework.

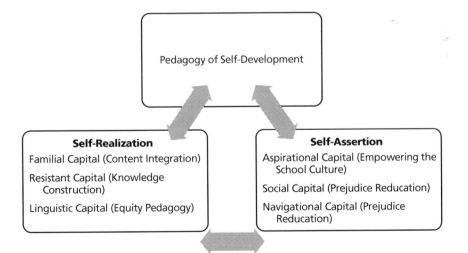

Figure 1.1   Pedagogy of self-development.

Thus, what we are advocating is for educators to commit to a pedagogy of self-development for the most vulnerable students who arrive at school without the "prerequisite" capital for achievement (McCray et al., 2010). The notion of pedagogy of self-development deals with educators recognizing and understanding that many CLD learners come to school with alternative forms of capital unlike the standard forms of social and cultural capital that many middle-class educators and school leaders have at their own disposal (Yosso, 2005).

According to Yosso (2005), CLD learners have alternative forms of capital that can be parlayed into academic achievement in schools. McCray et al. (2010), building on the notion of Yosso's (2005) alternative forms of capital, conflated them with the concept of pedagogy of self-development. The notion of pedagogy of self-development involves enhancing the sense of self-realization and self-assertion among CLD learners. J. A. Banks' (2001) five dimensions of multicultural education (i.e., content integration, knowledge construction, equity pedagogy, empowering the school culture, and prejudice reduction) can effectively undergird educators and school leaders' efforts to implement capital pluralism, wherein alternative forms of capital are recognized to enhance a pedagogy of self-development among CLD learners.

In order for students who have been traditionally marginalized in education to begin to make academic gains, educators and school leaders must begin to cultivate their students' sense of self-development. We emphasize academic self-development here because, in many instances, CLD students come to school with an overall high sense of self-esteem and self-efficacy (Foster, 2009). These students bring an enormous amount of alternative capital with them to the educational process. Such alternative capital needs to be channeled by educators and school leaders to enhance a sense of self and purpose among these student populations. Self-actualization increases among CLD students when the curriculum focuses on literacy and numeracy as well as the development of the entire student. A pedagogy of self-development is undergirded by the concepts of *self-realization* and *self-assertion.* McCray et al. (2010) elucidated that self-realization is "the way in which people make their dreams a reality, the way they feel about themselves, and how they understand the world around them" (p. 242). It is an awakening! We believe that self-realization among CLD learners is a prerequisite for self-assertion to materialize. McCray et al. found that self-assertion "deals with the way in which people prepare themselves for and seize opportunities" (p. 242). Thus, self-realization involves believing in the self and the possibility of making dreams come true, while self-assertion is the actualization of those beliefs. In other words, it is the taking advantage of an awakening.

When Barack Obama was elected President of the United States, there were many social pundits as well as educators who truly believed that the election would mean so much for students of color, particularly African American males. It was called the Obama Effect. The supposition was that the election of the first Black president would inspire a generation of young African American males to believe they too could one day become, if not the President of the United States, then the next senator, doctor, engineer, writer, or scientist. For far too long, the narrative in many communities of color has been one of doubt, pessimism, suspicion, and capitulation to the status quo (Alexander, 2010); inspiration toward academic and professional success is surely needed. But we caution that while the election of President Obama may have been a nascent opportunity for a counternarrative to be encouraged among CLD learners concerning their beliefs and goals, it will not in and of itself be sufficient to ensure a radical and substantive change in the academic aspirations of students of color. Such a cogent change can be induced, however, by caring, creative, and committed teachers and school leaders who have a thorough understanding of their student populations. This thorough understanding is undergirded by recognizing alternative forms of capital that students of color bring to the educational process and helping those students channel that capital into self-realization and self-assertion.

We believe the alternative forms of capital fit nicely with the notion of pedagogy of self-development. For African American students and students of color, self-realization is oftentimes manifested by three of Yosso's (2005) alternative forms of capital. When trying to develop a sense of purpose in life as well as developing a form of identity, students of color draw from their familial capital, resistant capital, and linguistic capital. Thus, school leaders and educators can have an enormous impact on cultivating or suppressing the self-realization of students of color via their critical understanding (or lack of understanding) of students familial, resistant, and linguistic capitals. We believe that J. A. Banks' (2001) multicultural education dimensions of content integration, knowledge construction, and equity pedagogy can be used to help students of color create meaning and purpose in their lives and enhance their self-realization. In far too many instances, students of color feel as if they are visitors within their own school and struggle daily to find meaning and a sense of identification. Such feelings resonate with CLD students due to underlying racial and class tension, which permeates the culture and climate of the school.

The other half of pedagogy of self-development—the notion of self-assertion—is undergirded by aspiration capital, social capital, and navigational capital. We have already gone into detail as to the meaning of these alternative forms of capital. We proffer that J. A. Banks' (2001) remaining two dimensions of multicultural education—empowering the school climate and prejudice reduction—can help parlay the aspirational capital, social capital, and navigational capital of students of color into a sense of self-assertion within the classroom and throughout their entire educative experience.

Conclusion

We opened this chapter with reports dealing with the academic achievement of African American students. These reports have shown us that we still have a long way to go if we are to ensure that African American students and other students of color are to reach self-actualization in life. As the reports have shown, many African American students and students of color continue to struggle academically, and there has not been a discernible decrease in the academic achievement gap between African American students and their White counterparts. The gap has increased in several areas. As we highlighted earlier in the chapter, in 2010, the Council of the Great City Schools produced a comprehensive report that concluded African American students are academically trailing their White, Asian, and Latino counterparts. The report indicated that African American students had lower graduation rates as well as lower overall academic achievement.

Alas, we are not convinced that the sole focus on literacy and numeracy along with shutting and reopening schools is in and of itself a remedy for academic success among African American students and other students of color. But we are keenly aware that politicians and plutocrats think otherwise. In what is seemingly the age of academic stagnation with regard to decreasing the academic achievement gap, politicians are struggling to find the magic formula for what works. We do not pretend to have anything close to a magical solution; however, what we do insist on is a renewed focus on multicultural education with an emphasis on students' self-realization and self-assertion. We advocate for educators and school leaders to recommit themselves to Banks' five dimensions of multicultural education in an effort to increase the *self-development* of all students.

This recommitment by educators and school leaders entails understanding how content integration, knowledge construction, equity pedagogy, prejudice reduction, and empowering the school culture (Banks' five dimensions of multicultural education) can parlay Yosso's (2005) alternative forms of capital among students of color—familial, resistant, linguistic, aspirational, social, and navigational—into a sense of self-realization and self-assertion in CLD students. We do not believe that a pedagogy of self-development among students of color can exist if the alternative forms of capital in students of color are not respected and cultivated within the school, as well as in the classroom. School leaders should help faculty and staff by providing authentic workshops dealing with Banks' five dimensions, particularly workshops dealing with teaching and learning with an emphasis on content integration, knowledge construction, and equity pedagogy. These workshops can highlight how such dimensions are connected to Yosso's alternative forms of capital.

Just as school leaders can offer professional development dealing with teaching and learning, they should also offer training to faculty on how to ensure that the classroom is free from racial and class hostility, and on cultivating a climate conducive to empowering all students. This form of training is tantamount to J. A. Banks' (2001) prejudice reduction and empowering the school culture. If schools are to make strides in the 21st century in closing the academic achievement gap between African American students and their White counterparts, school leaders and educators must gain an understanding of how to construct the school curricula to deliver a pedagogy for the development of all students.

2

Bridging the Gap

Going Beyond Traditional Thought

In order for multicultural education to continue to have relevancy in the 21st century, educators and school leaders must begin to practice its edicts in earnest. In Chapter 1, we briefly discussed the history and origin of multicultural education. We indicated that multicultural education came to fruition during the late '60s and early '70s in concert with the Civil Rights Movement and the Women's Movement. In essence, Black scholars such as the venerable Cater G. Woodson began to conduct content audits on what was being taught to many African American students. Woodson discovered through his research that the curricula in many schools throughout the United States at this time were leaving out significant contributions by people of color.

The lack of diverse content being offered to an increasingly diverse student population was the ultimate catalyst for what is today called multicultural education. Today, the basic premise of multiculturalism entails an approach that promotes cultural pluralism by ensuring that all students, regardless of their race, gender, sexual orientation, mental and physical

School Leadership in a Diverse Society, pages 23–42
Copyright © 2014 by Information Age Publishing
All rights of reproduction in any form reserved.

ability, socioeconomic status, and religion, have an equal opportunity to learn in school by changing the total educational environment (J. A. Banks, 2001; Blumenfeld & Raymond, 2000; Sleeter & Grant, 1987).

This *diktat* of multicultural education seems very plausible and doable for educators and school leaders to implement. Despite multiculturalists' best attempts to make multiculturalism a viable curricula for students, there are many in the field of education who still feel that multiculturalism is either inadequate for the task at hand or is an impediment in the educative process (McCray et al., 2004). This latter argument is usually couched in the idea that multiculturalism is a distraction from real learning (i.e., literacy and numeracy) (McCray et al., 2004). The former argument is made by those who feel that multicultural education has become too diluted to have an impact on the numerous issues faced by students who are disempowered in the educational process. At the epicenter of this argument is that multicultural education has become coopted by would-be detractors, and it is now little more than a celebratory piece of the curriculum to make students, faculty, and staff feel good (Gorski, 2006). As was mentioned in Chapter 1, Dantley (2002) talked about these concerns and strongly insisted that for multicultural education to once again achieve its relevancy, it must "openly identify oppression and struggle against it" (p. 540). Thus, in this chapter, we continue our efforts to show that not only does multicultural education still have relevancy, but it is strongly needed to address the plethora of issues associated with the numerous disenfranchised students that educators and school leaders readily encounter.

When most educators think of multicultural education, for the most part, they normally think of the first phase of its origin—the Ethnic Studies stage, which was referenced in Chapter 1. This period of multicultural education consisted of scholars such as Carter G. Woodson advocating for students of color to be exposed to a more comprehensive curriculum (i.e., content reflective of their heritage) within their educational experience (J. A. Banks, 1996). Unfortunately, educators and school leaders tend to conflate the celebratory piece of multicultural education with content integration (usually on a specific day or month) and thus are satisfied with their anemic efforts.

Multicultural Education in the 21st Century

With such a weak delivery of multicultural education by educators and school leaders, it is understandable why some scholars have become disenchanted with multiculturalism and feel the need to move on to other critical theories to enhance educational opportunities for culturally and linguistically diverse (CLD) learners (McCray, 2010). But we believe that multicultural education is still a viable method to not only improve learning for all students but to also cultivate a school climate (McCray et al., 2006) in which students feel safe and are empowered to reach a sense of self-actualization (Wright & Tolan, 2009). In Chapter 1, we conveyed how multicultural education can be used to increase students' *self-assertion* and *self-realization*, leading to a *pedagogy of self-development*, especially among African American students and other CLD learners.

But in this chapter, we would like to show that multicultural education can also be useful for enhancing the self-assertion and self-realization of other marginalized students. Educators and school leaders need to come to the understanding that multicultural education is not simply meant for African American students and other students of color, but it is meant to help all students academically and socially, especially as the United States becomes more socially and culturally diverse than ever before in its history (McLaren, 1997). Some educators and school leaders tend to believe that multicultural education benefits only certain groups and does not necessarily benefit the masses (McCray et al., 2004; Gay, 1995). However, these individuals have greatly missed the mark concerning the true purposes of multicultural education. A multicultural curricula benefits all students in helping our society become a better place to live (Houser, 1996).

We believe one way in which multicultural education benefits all students is by giving school leaders and educators the ability to structure the school and classroom climate in ways to promote a pedagogy of self-development—the self-assertion and self-realization of students. A pedagogy of self-development among student does not take place when there is an absence of meaningful contact between students who are different culturally as well as socially. Students' self-assertion and self-realization are able to materialize as a result of authentic interaction with their peers and teachers. Therefore, school leaders and educators can ill afford to create conditions in which *de facto* segregation among students is the school norm. Such segregation within the school and classroom occurs when educators implicitly as well as explicitly create conditions and opportunities to separate students who bring vastly different social and cultural capital with them to school (Ferguson, 2001).

Authentic Contact Reduces Prejudice

One of the underpinnings of multicultural education is G. W. Allport's (1954) notion of contact hypothesis. In 1954, psychologist Gordon Willard Allport developed the contact hypothesis, which stated that contact among students of different races could greatly reduce the preconceived notions that students have of one another. It is worth pointing out that Allport's contact hypothesis coincided with the famous Supreme Court case, *Brown v. Board of Education*, the decision that would eventually lead to the dismantling of legalized segregation. According to Allport, respect and morale can be accomplished among different racial groups when contact is based on four specific circumstances: (a) equal status, (b) cooperation rather competition, (c) sanctions by authorities such as teachers and administrators, and (d) interpersonal interactions in which students become acquainted as individuals.

Wittig and Grant-Thompson (1998) concluded that Allport's contact hypothesis (1954) has been one of "the most researched psychological principles for reducing interracial prejudice" (p. 798). Thus, we also believe that Allport's contact hypothesis can help improve the climate and culture of the school by promoting authentic and positive interaction among not only different racial and ethnic groups but also among students who tend to be labeled as a target group (McCray et al., 2006). Harro (2000) defined target groups as the students of color, female students, students with different sexual orientation and religious beliefs, as well as those students from lower socioeconomic backgrounds. Hardiman and Jackson (1997) opined that these aforementioned groups of students are the exploited and disenfranchised. It is well documented throughout the research how target groups are sometimes at a disadvantage academically due to racist, classist, sexist, and homophobic policies. Over the past few years, there have been numerous incidents highlighting the daily humiliation faced by targeted students in the educative process as a result of such polices, as well as many educators' ineptitude in dealing with a diverse student population.

The issue of bullying has been at the forefront of everyone's mind due to the number of students who have committed suicide as a result of severe harassment in what is supposedly their safe haven—the schools they attend daily. Bullying in school was brought to the national stage in 2011 when President Obama hosted a conference on the issue. The purpose of this forum was to engage the public on what the President considered a serious issue that schools needed to confront. During this event, the President admitted that he too experienced bullying in school and felt the need to start a national dialogue on the issue.

Researchers (Waters, 2011; Young, Nelson, Hottle, Warburton, & Young 2011) have found that the number of suicides have increased exponentially due to the severity of bullying in schools. It is unfortunate that the very places that are supposed to increase students' sense of self-esteem and self-efficacy have now become places where many students ironically feel ostracized and threatened by their peers. In the 21st century, it is abhorrent that there are students who are still not able to attend school without being disliked and demeaned because of their cultural or social background. We believe that just as multicultural education can have an impact on students of color from a pedagogy of self-development standpoint, it can also be used to confront the issue of students who experience such disenfranchisement.

Bullying Defined

Dan Olweus, who was one of the pioneers in bullying research, defined bullying as the "verbal or physical actions that cause physical or psychological harm, are repeated over time, and occur in a relationship of unequal power" (as cited in Waters, 2011, p. 7). When most people think of bullying, they usually think of physical harm and abuse committed by students who are usually bigger and stronger than their peers. However, bullies can also cause severe psychological harm by verbally abusing others. Thus, with this form of bullying, the size of the bully may or may not be an issue. For instance, Young et al. (2011) have found that oftentimes bullying comes in the form of *relational aggression*. Young et al. opined that this form of bullying is just as pervasive in our schools but more difficult to detect due to the fact that it is ostensibly benevolent and is considered somewhat of a rite of passage for all students. This type of harassment involves "harm within relationships caused by covert bullying or manipulative behavior" (p. 24). It also involves but is not limited to students ostracizing another particular student from his or her social group as well as spreading rumors of the student via email, Facebook, Twitter, and other social network sites. "Relational aggression was viewed as a normal part of the socialization process. However, relational aggression may create just as much or even more damage than physical aggression . . . and should be considered an important focus of bullying and aggression and intervention" (p. 25).

President Obama echoed this sentiment concerning the need to debunk the notion that students' harassing of other students is simply a process of navigating adolescence. He opined at his White House conference that the purpose of the convening was to debunk the myth that bullying is simply a passive rite of passage in the growing-up process of young students. (Calms, 2011).

Harvey Milk Institute

Regardless of whether bullying takes the form of physical abuse or psychological terror, it is an act of aggression that needs to be ameliorated in order for all students to have an opportunity to achieve. It is simply unacceptable for students to be terrorized within their own schools. This notion of students being threatened and intimidated within a supposedly safe haven is what led New York City to open the Harvey Milk Institute, which is a school located in the East Village in Manhattan (Reid, 2003). The school's mission and vision are undergirded by the premise that it is a place where students who are not heterosexual can attend and feel safe from bullying, whether psychological or physical.

Obviously, we applaud the effort of school officials and policymakers to create such a school for gay, lesbian, bisexual, and transgendered students. However, we are somewhat discouraged that such a school was needed due to the ineffectiveness of school leaders and educators at other schools within the city to provide a safe learning environment for this student population. It was widely acknowledge that the reason the Harvey Milk Institute was created was that there were several students being bullied at their regular schools. We commend the city school administrators of New York for being proactive with regard to abating the physical and psychological terror that many gay and lesbian students face on a daily basis. But we find it very difficult to believe that school leaders cannot protect students from this type of harassment.

Regardless of a student's sexual orientation, race, ethnicity, gender, or religious status, he or she should be able to attend school without being subjected to physical and psychological abuse. Dyson (2009) has found that "All of us have to confront the sexism, misogyny, patriarchy, and homophobia that are deeply rooted in our culture" (p. 241). School officials and educators cannot afford to acquiesce to the notion that *boys will be boys* when it comes to physical and psychological harassment or intimidation within the school. Those who act *in loco parentis* (i.e., in lieu of the parents) have to become diligent with regard to saving our children from unnecessary harassment, which can have an impact on their lives for years to come. Dyson has found that the "justification for the social stigma of homosexuality—and in some cases, for the violence expressed toward gay and lesbian people—is taken for granted in many quarters of the culture" (p. 249).

Utilizing Multicultural Education for Anti-Bullying

The edicts of multicultural education can have a major role in helping to eradicate some of the aforementioned issues that are plaguing diverse student populations. The problem, as we mentioned earlier, is that multicultural education is losing some of its appeal with educators as well as scholars. To us, this is somewhat troubling considering that multicultural education was in the forefront of naming and labeling social injustices that were occurring within the field of education among CLD students. Ergo, we feel that multicultural education can be a great asset to educators in the field who are dealing with any form of heterogeneity in their schools. Dr. Martin Luther King Jr. once highlighted the urgent need for mutual interaction among diverse populations. Dr. King believed that "all life is interrelated. We are all caught up in an inescapable network of mutuality tied in a single garment of destiny. Whatever affects one indirectly, affects all directly" (as cited in Washington, 1991, p. 254).

This quote by Dr. King is appropriate in the sense that it recognizes the need for interdependence among individuals in order to accomplish objectives and goals, whether it is within an organizational setting, small groups, or personal interactions. Why is the notion of cultivating interdependent relationships of vital importance in today's society? We believe that the answer to this question lies in the notion that as our society becomes more interdependent (Friedman, 2005), there is an increasing need for the dissipation of prejudice toward one another. And when students are bullied and harassed because of their sexual orientation, aesthetic appeal, religious beliefs, and other trivial reasons for which they have no control, the interdependence that Dr. King eloquently spoke of is placed at risk among an increasingly diverse student population—students who will eventually become adults without an appreciation of Dr. King's notion of mutuality for one's neighbor.

When it comes to the appreciation of the heterogeneity found within our schools and society, McCray and Beachum (2010) reminded us the following:

> Just as it seemed that America was making significant progress in dealing with issues of racism, sexism, and other forms of bigotry, in recent years there have been a plethora of issues that have arisen to remind us that we still need multicultural education to fight intolerance and prejudice. (p. 2)

The bullying that many students have to deal with on a daily basis as a result of issues such as homophobia and aestheticism can be eradicated if school leaders and educators create a school climate and culture that is free from intimidation. When we speak of aestheticism, we are referring to the notion that students are discriminated against due to their aesthetic appeal (see McCray, Beachum, and Richardson, 2008). This lack of aesthetic appeal can be undergirded by a student's height, weight, pigmentation, hair texture, or attire.

In Chapter 1, we mentioned the concepts, *prejudice reduction* and *empowering the school culture* with regard to cultivating a sense of self-assertion among CLD learners. We indicated that prejudice reduction occurs when educators and school leaders formulate a school culture and classroom climate to assist students in reducing any negative attitude and biases they might have against one another. When we broached this concept in Chapter 1, we did it from the lens of racial and ethnic biases. However, we also believe that educators and school leaders should also have a keen understanding of bullying that occurs in schools as a result of homophobia and aestheticism. Very few scholars have applied Bank's notion of prejudice reduction when considering how to reduce the amount of prejudice gay and lesbian students experience from their heterosexual counterparts as well as the cruelty experienced by those who are perceived to lack a certain aesthetic capital. In far too many instances, these students are confronted daily with psychological and physical abuse from their peers. And when it comes to such abuses, educators and school leaders must be diligent in cultivating a school climate and culture that is conducive to all students, regardless of their sexual orientation or any other form of identity.

Bullying is a Form Discrimination

In order to reduce the prejudice that many students are exposed to in schools, we offer Feagin and Feagin's (1978) framework for dealing with racism, prejudice, and discrimination in the organization. Just as Feagin and Feagin's framework helped organizations actively confront the issues of racism and discrimination, we also believe that such a framework can help schools deal with the issues of classism, aestheticism, and homophobia. Feagin and Feagin understood that if leaders of organizations were to increase their productivity as their organizations were becoming more diverse, it was imperative for these leaders to respond to such diversity in an appreciate manner. Organizational behaviorist Taylor Cox also recognized that in order for organizations to function effectively and efficiently with an increasing amount of cultural diversity, they must transform their organizations into multicultural organizations. Cox (1994) found that multicultural organizations are committed to going from homogeneous recruitment and staffing to a more heterogeneous selection process, harnessing the heterogeneity into increased productivity.

According to Dantley (2009), models such as Feagin and Feagin (1978) can help reduce prejudice and discrimination within the organization and also increase the productivity of individuals while providing a greater sense of job satisfaction. Dantley also opined that the Feagin and Feagin model can be utilized in educational organizations to help educational leaders understand the issues of racism and classism and appropriately deal with the potential discrimination that comes with it. The ultimate goal, according to Dantley, is an educational reconstruction that is undergirded by egalitarian principles. If school leaders are going to ensure that all students are able to participate in the educative process, there has to be a commitment to cultivating a school climate and culture free of bigotry and discrimination. Feagin and Feagin's notion of organizational discrimination identifies four forms of discrimination that occur within the organization as a result racism.

The four types of discriminations that were identified by Feagin and Feagin (1978) are as follows: (a) isolated discrimination, (b) small group discrimination, (c) direct institutionalized discrimination, (d) indirect institutionalized discrimination. Once again, Feagin and Feagin identified these types of discrimination found within organizations as they relate to racism. But in concert with Dantley (2009), we also believe that the Feagin and Feagin model can help school leaders with issues such as student harassment and bullying. Educators and school leaders can use Feagin and Feagin's model of organizational discrimination to effectively diminish the amount of bullying that takes place in the educative process.

The bullying that exists in schools is undergirded by biases and prejudices against those who are perceived as different from the rest of the student population (i.e., gays and lesbians, those from impoverished backgrounds, the "weak" and "timid," as well as those who are not considered aesthetically appealing). Such differences among a student population, along with a school culture undergirded by an implicit code of bigotry, can lead to implicit approval for students to bully those who are different. As was alluded to earlier in this chapter, the issue of school bullying is serious, with drastic ramifications on a generation of students who fall into a target group. It is now time for school officials to seriously address students who are subjected to a hostile environment due to circumstances beyond their control. Our supposition is that school officials must begin to employ J. A. Banks' (2011) precepts of multicultural education along with Feagin and Feagin's (1978) notion of organizational discrimination to improve the learning conditions of many students who are experiencing psychological trauma daily.

In Chapter 1, we discussed James Banks' (2001) five dimensions of multicultural education. The five dimensions were *equity pedagogy, content integration, knowledge construction, prejudice reduction,* and *empowering the school culture.* Two of Banks' dimensions of multicultural education, *prejudice reduction* and *empowering the school culture,* combined with Feagin's and Feagin's (1978) notion of organizational discrimination, can be utilized by educators and school leaders to help stop senseless discrimination among students—the harassment that is leading to them dropping out of school and taking their own lives.

The first level of discrimination that occurs within an organization, according to Feagin and Feagin (1978), is isolated discrimination. Feagin and Feagin found that isolated discrimination occurs in an organization when a member of the organization has gone "rogue" from the by-the-book mission of the organization. McCray and Beachum (2011b) elucidated that isolated discrimination occurs in the educational process when the individual educator engages in a form of informal discrimination toward students who may not have the prerequisite social and cultural capital. Thus, we would like to expand the notion of isolated discrimination in the context of bullying. In many instances, isolated discrimination in the form of bullying occurs on the student-to-student level. McCray and Beachum (2010) have found that in many instances, students experience discrimination at this level due to inherent characteristics that they bring to school with them.

As we mentioned earlier, when it comes to discrimination, students as well as adults oftentimes fall within two categories, depending on their inherent characteristics (i.e., race, gender, sexual orientation, religious affiliation, class status, etc.). These two characteristics are *target groups* and *agent groups*. Once again, the target groups are composed of individuals whose inherent characteristics make them more susceptible to discrimination, while agent groups are made up of individuals who are more likely to benefit from their inherent characteristics within society as well as the school (Harro, 2000). At the student-to-student level, students often take the opportunity to exploit other individuals for personal gains. This is usually done outside the purview of educators, who are either too busy with other duties to pay attention to the bullying or have decided to look the other way because of a false understanding of a pseudo *rites of passage* or an acquiescence to the axiom "Boys will be boys." Either way, it is a mistake for educators to not focus on one-on-one bullying or discrimination by students and to attribute it to some form of *rites of passage* or a false *truism* regarding how students are ultimately going to behave.

The second form of discrimination that was identified by Feagin and Feagin (1978) that occurs within an organization is *small group discrimination*. McCray and Beachum (2011b) described *small group discrimination* found among teachers as the hegemony that is found within concentric group(s) who all share the same beliefs, attitudes, and dispositions that are undergirded by racist and classist perspectives, which further reinforce the isolation of poor students and students of color who have not fallen in line with school officials' level of expectations. Here, we are describing how educators in many instances tend to engage in small group discrimination toward students wherein a collision of values and culture might exist. We also believe that small group discrimination in the educative process occurs at the student level as well. One example of small group discrimination is the controversy that took place in Jena, Louisiana, in 2006 when six Black teenagers were charged with assaulting a White teenager. It was later revealed that racial tension had been building as a result of a noose being placed in a tree to intimidate Black teenagers from socializing in the shade of that tree. The incident made national news and created outrage all across the country. In this particular incident, the bullying actually came from both sides. The White teenager was probably not acting alone when he decided to hang the noose in the tree to intimidate the Black students. Also, the Black students' response to the bullying probably exacerbated an already tense situation. Undoubtedly, both groups were engaging in what Feagin and Feagin (1978) called small group discrimination. In both instances, there was explicit and implicit reliance on an assembly of students in order to bully other students who were perceived as different or powerless.

With regard to the Jena situation, the White student made the conscious decision to expose the African American students to a symbol that represents the ultimate terror and brutality for Blacks. Likewise, when the African American students retaliated against the perpetrator, it led to the White student being hospitalized as a result of the number of students who were outraged at his actions and decided to join in on the fight (McCray & Beachum, 2010). Thus, we believe this example is a perfect illustration of group discrimination that occurs in the educative process among students. In the following chapter, we provide a case that highlights another issue concerning small group discrimination. Alas, just as educators and educational leaders are oftentimes implicitly complicit in one-on-one discrimination, as in looking the other way or rationalizing such behavior as natural, school officials are often complicit in student small group discrimination as well. Admittedly, when it comes to small group discrimination, educators and school leaders usually make themselves more aware of such activities that are occurring within the school. In many instances, educators and school leaders are aware that small group discrimination left unaddressed can lead to mass disturbances within the school as well as violence, such as in the Jena episode.

Another example of small group discrimination and bullying that took place within school is the harassment of a female student in Northampton, Massachusetts, a few years ago. As a result of the relentless bullying that a young female student endured in school when she moved with her family from Ireland to Massachusetts, anti-bullying legislation was passed in the state of Massachusetts to try to prevent further intimidation and harassment in school. The young 15-year-old student, Phoebe Prince, was bullied so severely in school by other students that she eventually committed suicide. Nine teenagers were charged with Phoebe's death. These nine teenagers faced an array of charges that included assault, criminal harassment, violation of civil rights resulting in injury, disturbance of school assembly, and stalking. Some in the group also face statutory rape charges as well. We commend the state of Massachusetts for enacting legislation to try to curb school bullying. Although we find it extremely disturbing that school officials might have known about the bullying that this young lady was being exposed to while at school. And unfortunately, there are countless other examples across the nation in which students have taken their own lives due to small group discrimination and harassment.

Schools are supposed to be safe havens for children—many who come to get away from myriad issues and problems they might face in their respective communities. It is unfortunate that in many instances students find themselves on the receiving end of harassment in places (i.e., the school) that are supposed to help cultivate a sense of self-realization and self-assertion. This is truly one of the unfortunate realities of the educative process for students who are vulnerable to such persecution and harassment. Up to now we have talked about the unfortunate reality of bullying with regard to one-on-one student harassment and discrimination as well as small group bullying and discrimination. Another one of Feagin and Feagin's (1978) concepts of discrimination we believe is appropriate to discuss when talking about the issue of student bullying is the notion of indirect institutionalized discrimination.

Here, we suggest that indirect institutionalized discrimination is the catalyst for the aforementioned forms of discrimination that we have covered (i.e., isolated discrimination and small group discrimination). The concept of indirect institutionalized discrimination is undergirded by the notion that the school is complicit in any form of harassment or bullying target students experience. We recognize that such a supposition seems ironic. After all, as we conveyed earlier, schools are supposed to be a place where cogent learning takes place and where students are afforded the opportunity to realize and achieve their dreams. McCray and Beachum have found that this form of discrimination takes place when seemingly innocent practices and procedures produce a school atmosphere that is undergirded by a sense of bigotry.

These seemingly innocent practices are usually codified by educators and school officials not being diligent enough in forming policies and procedures to deter students from unnecessary harassment and discrimination. In many instances, educators and school officials choose not to place as a high priority the need to cultivate a school culture and climate that promotes harmony and a cohesive coexistence among students who are coming from diverse backgrounds. Yosso (2005) has proffered that in many cases, "schools most often oppress and marginalize while they maintain the potential to emancipate and empower" (p. 74). Likewise, McCray and Beachum (2010) have conveyed that because of the increasing amount of social and cultural diversity occurring in our society and schools, "school officials must be cognizant of the oppressive policies that are embedded within [their] schools" (p. 3). In addition, McCray and Beachum went to on to proffer that "oppressive policies may instill in students who belong to certain disenfranchised or marginalized groups a feeling of dejection, rejection, and unsteadiness" (p. 3). And Dantley (2009) has also opined that certain rituals and rites of passage in schools inadvertently lead to a school climate and culture in which there is a lack of respect among student populations. Thus, Dantley's assertion underscores the need to constantly critique school policies and procedures to prevent the continued marginalization of students.

A perfect example of indirect institutionalized discrimination is the fluid situation in the Anoka-Hennepin School District, which is the largest school district in Minnesota. In 2011, a group of former and current students from the Anoka-Hennepin District brought a suit against the district complaining that the district's sexual orientation neutrality policy was doing severe damage to students who were gay, lesbian, or bisexual. The students' argument was that the policy prohibits teachers from engaging students in dialogue surrounding issues that are of critical importance to the gay and lesbian student population. The plaintiffs believed that by educators and school officials not creating teachable moments in the classroom concerning issues of same-sex dating, they cultivated a school culture and climate in which gay and lesbian students (i.e., target students) are more prone to being on the receiving end of harassment, bullying, and discrimination. The plaintiffs also argued that the Anoka-Hennepin same-sex neutrality policy led to the suicide of at least six students in a 2-year time span (2009–2011). Mary Bauer, the legal director for the Southern Poverty Law Center, summed up the Anoka-Hennepin policy very succinctly. According to Ms. Bauer, "This policy sends the message to kids that who they are is not okay" (Smith, 2011).

As we mentioned earlier, another example of indirect institutionalized discrimination in our schools involves gay and lesbian students who have been implicitly ushered out of their home schools (i.e., the New York Public Schools) into the Harvey Milk Institute in order to prevent them from being bullied and discriminated against. Even though school and city officials had the best interest of the students in mind, there is something ominously disturbing about students having to leave a heterogeneous student body population for a more homogenous one in order to feel safe. By school leaders, educators, and school officials failing to ensure that all students, regardless of their sexual orientation, feel a sense of empowerment in the school, indirect institutionalized discrimination was the cause of many of the students moving to Harvey Milk. Whether students in school are confronting isolated bullying and discrimination, group discrimination, or indirect institutionalized discrimination, educators and school officials have an obligation to ensure that situations like the Jena, Louisiana, episode, and the Phoebe Prince case are removed from the culture of the school.

Practical Suggestions to Combat Bullying

In order for student bullying, harassment, and discrimination to be ameliorated in our schools, educators and school leaders have to ensure that policies as well as the school culture and climate reflect an atmosphere of trust, respect, and high morale for all students regardless of their circumstances (McCray et al., 2006). As we indicated earlier in this chapter, we believe that multicultural education is a curricular approach to ensure that all students are able to learn in an environment that is free from bigotry and prejudice regardless of their social or cultural characteristics. Oftentimes a multicultural approach is not considered by school officials and educators when dealing with student harassment, bullying, and discrimination if it is not undergirded by issues dealing with race and ethnicity, such as the student racial confrontation in Jena, Louisiana. The line of reasoning espoused by educators and school leaders that multicultural education is somewhat anemic or inadequate for the dissipation of student harassment, discrimination, or bullying is very problematic. As we have indicated before, multicultural education is a curricula approach that promotes cultural pluralism by ensuring that all CLD learners are free from harassment and discrimination regardless of any target characteristic (J. A. Banks, 2001; Blumenfeld & Raymond, 2000; Sleeter & Grant, 1987).

Multicultural education is an appropriate curricular approach for ensuring that isolated discrimination, group discrimination, and indirect institutionalized discrimination are not prevalent within the culture of the school. Here we offer a school climate, educational, and theoretical approach to multicultural education to ensure a healthy school culture is cultivated with the effect of a dramatic decrease in the number of students who are victims of harassment, discrimination, and bullying within the school. Throughout this chapter we have talked about the number of ways in which students are bullied in school (i.e., isolated discrimination, group discrimination, and indirect institutionalized discrimination). We proffer that in order for student-to-student harassment to decrease, it has to start at the top. This means that educators and school officials must be willing to engage in the inquiries concerning what kind of education they are trying to deliver to students in an increasingly diverse society.

As we indicated in Chapter 1, the United States is becoming more socially and culturally diverse than ever before in its history. When we previously talked about the increasing heterogeneity in the United States, we usually limited our focus of diversity to race and ethnicity. Today, in addition to the increasing racial and ethnic diversity that is occurring within our society, there is also a sizable amount of religious diversity as well as sexual orientation diversity that is shaping the cultural and social landscape of the United States. By the time this book is published, the United States Supreme Court will (perhaps) make one of the most important rulings in the last half century—the ruling on same-sex marriage. Students, whether they are embedded in a homogenous or heterogeneous school environment, are going to, more often than not, come in contact with this increasing diversity once they leave their immediate surroundings. Ironically, this is one of the centerpieces of multicultural education—the idea that students should be prepared to deal with the increasing amount of diversity once they "get out into the real world."

McCray and Beachum (2010) argued that the theoretical value of multicultural education is an effective approach to ensuring that students are prepared to deal with the diversity they will encounter once they leave their surroundings. According to McCray and Beachum, "The theoretical perspective entails the belief that multicultural education is for all students, elevates students' self-esteem, is embedded in cultural pluralism, and recognizes the social, political, and economic community and social construct for students" (p. 2). Here, McCray and Beachum have emphatically indicated that multicultural education can benefit all students and is not just simply for students of color. Educators and school leaders make a critical mistake in their conceptualization of multicultural education when they assume it is only for students of color. Likewise, the theoretical perspective of multicultural education enhances students' self-esteem—something that is absolutely crucial in many of our schools that have students who are potential targets as a result of their religious views, race and ethnicity, sexual orientation, and aesthetic appeal. In far too many instances, draconian school policies and procedures can negatively impact students' self-esteem. In Chapter 1, we talked about the idea of a pedagogy of self-development, in which educators and school leaders enhance students' sense of self-realization and self-assertion by recognizing alternative forms of capital students have at their disposal. Many of our students who are potential targets for harassment and bullying are hurting badly and are psychologically scarred from daily abuse, whether from within their own communities or at school.

The theoretical perspective of multicultural education recognizes this form of psychological scarring and is a viable approach to its amelioration. But educators and school officials must become cognizant of what students are going through on a daily basis. In addition to raising students' self-realization and self-assertion, the theoretical perspective demands that the school culture and climate are based on the notion of cultural pluralism. Thus, school leaders must create environments that promote cultural pluralism and provide every student with an opportunity to attain her or his maximum potential. M. M. Gordon (1978) found that "Cultural pluralism involves giving and taking and, more importantly, the sharing of and mutual respect for ideas, customs and values" (p. 64). Cox (1994) further stated, "Pluralism refers to a two-way learning and adaptation process in which both the organization and entering members from various cultural backgrounds change to some degree to reflect the cultural norms and values of the other" (p. 167). Once again, we return to Yosso's (2005) notion of alternative forms of capital. We find it very problematic for cultural pluralism to exist within the school if educators and school leaders do not value the experiences that students bring with them into the educative process.

Finally, the theoretical perspective of multicultural education also requires educators and school officials to think big concerning students' experiences inside the classroom as well as outside of the school. This is what undergirds the social, political, and economic aspects of the theoretical perspective. Sleeter (1996) raised concerns that some multicultural theorists have begun to compromise the basic foundation of multicultural education in order to appease opponents who intend to maintain the status quo. Thus, one of the main goals of multicultural education, from a theoretical perspective, is to challenge the social, economic, and political status quo, especially when any form of oppression is implicitly or explicitly embedded in such a status quo.

Thus, when school educators and school leaders refuse to acknowledge the potential harm of neutrality-based school policies regarding gays and lesbians or fail to cultivate a school climate in which gays and lesbians can safely navigate from class to class without the fear of being harassed or bullied, they implicitly condone the devastating harm this student population faces. The same is true for the students in the Jena incident that we talked about earlier. Situations like this can be avoided if educators and school leaders are diligent in addressing the need to embed cultural pluralism into the school climate and culture.

A cogent school climate and culture that is based on cultural pluralism is an absolute necessity for ensuring that indirect institutionalized discrimination, group discrimination and isolated discrimination are eliminated from within the school. McCray et al. (2006) have found that it is the school leader who is charged with the task of cultivating a positive school culture and climate for all students to succeed. And this entails the need to cultivate school policies that take into consideration the socially and culturally diverse student populations within the school. "A robust school culture does not happen by accident. Rather it is the result of careful planning, ongoing monitoring, and skillful leadership. [And] the principal, . . . as leader of the school is strategically positioned to shape those characteristics" (Marriot, 2001, p. 75).

With regard to the planning process, school leaders should have a thorough understanding of any discrepancies and disconnects that exist within school climate (i.e., day-to-day interactions) and where he or she wishes the school culture to be in the immediate future. As Marriot (2001) indicated, this entails effective leadership and constant monitoring of the school climate in order to cultivate an atmosphere that is free from harassment and discrimination. When it comes to student bullying, the end goal of this type of leadership is for all students to feel as if the school culture is a space in which they feel respected, have a high sense of morale, and are trusting of school leaders, educators, and their fellow classmates. The notion of all students feeling a sense of trust, respect, and high morale within the school is a major underpinning of multicultural education as it relates to establishing a strong school culture.

As we stated earlier, the basic premise of the contact hypothesis was that diverse individuals, culturally as well as socially, would be more receptive to one another if they had more meaningful and authentic contact. In Beverly Daniel Tatum's book, *Why Are All the Black Kids Sitting Together in the Cafeteria*, (Tatum, 1997) she points out that in many instances, students tend to self-segregate themselves. This self-segregation tends to lead to students not having the opportunity to make meaningful connections with individuals who may be different from themselves. McCray et al. (2006) have opined that by school leaders and educators ensuring that students have the opportunity for meaningful contact is a way to increase respect, high morale, and trust among not only the students but also among students and their teachers as well. In addition, Diaz-Lazaro and Cohen (2001) found that in a comprehensive literature review involving the contact hypothesis, Allport's (1954) theory seemed to be recognized the most for reducing prejudice among those who are seen as different. Thus, in order for meaningful contact to be accomplished, school leaders and educators should work diligently to cultivate a school climate and culture that ensures equal status among all students. Furthermore, it should be undergirded by a sense of cooperation rather than competition, which is sanctioned by the educators and school officials themselves. Finally, educators and school leaders should work to create an environment in which interpersonal interactions among students flourish, thus allowing them to become better acquainted as individuals.

Educational Perspective

In the spirit of thinking outside of the box, we proffer here that in order to reduce student bullying, especially at the isolated and group discrimination levels, the educational perspective—undergirded by J. A. Banks' (1995) content integration—should be utilized by educators in their classrooms. The educational perspective of multicultural education is operationalized here as the extent to which what is taught in the classroom allows students to academically achieve to their fullest capacity.

Previously, we talked about the educational perspective (i.e., *content integration, knowledge construction,* and *equity pedagogy*) as a conceptual framework for the educational perspective (McCray et al., 2006). Here we offer the dimension of *content integration* as way to dissipate the notion of isolated bullying and group discrimination bullying. J. A. Banks' (2001) dimension of *content integration* requires of the educator the use material from different cultures and groups to make a lesson a more meaningful experience. A good example for educators to pull from as it relates to utilizing content integration to reduce student discrimination, harassment, and bullying is the movie *Freedom Writers.* In this very provocative movie dealing with inner-city students and the notion of tragicomic hope (West, 2004), there is a scene that succinctly illustrates how educators can use *content integration* to reduce student harassment. In this particular scene, a Latino student draws a caricature of a Black student that harkens back to days of Jim Crow propaganda. The Latino student then proceeds to pass the picture to the Black student who becomes visibly shaken by the image. To her credit, the teacher in the movie immediately intervenes. She then proceeds to recalibrate her pedagogy and gives the students a history lesson on how this picture was not far removed from the type of propaganda use by the Nazis to intimidate, threaten, and devalue the Jewish populations prior to and during World War II. The teacher wanted the students to understand a few points. First, such images are extremely hurtful and painful to those on the receiving end. Second, what starts out as immature microteasing can spiral into something larger wherein entire groups of people are systematically devalued. In the case of the Nazi propaganda, it led to one of the greatest atrocities in modern history.

It was a powerful scene in the film, illustrating that educators and school leaders can't afford to capitulate to the notion of teaching strictly to the test at the cost of giving up on teachable moments such as the one in the film. Content integration, if used properly, can be a powerful approach in reducing the type of activities we have seen Jena, Louisiana, and Massachusetts, where students feel disempowered and disconnected from the very places that are supposed to nourish their minds and prepare them for a life of fulfillment.

Conclusion

Throughout this chapter, we have discussed ways in which students are exposed to bullying, harassment, and discrimination in school. Students who are potential targets due to their race, ethnicity, religious affiliation, aesthetic appearance, and sexual orientation (just to name a few) are vulnerable to isolated discrimination as well as group discrimination. Isolated discrimination occurs when a student who feels empowered decides to harass another student who is perhaps more vulnerable due to such aforementioned characteristics. In many instances, this is looked upon by educators and school officials as a simple rite of passage that students must go through in their journey through the educative process. Thus, educators seemingly turn a blind eye to the harassment or do not take it seriously with regard to any punitive measures toward the perpetuator. The other form of bullying or discrimination that occurs within the school is group discrimination. This form of harassment occurs when a number of students engage in verbal, physical, or psychological terror against students who appear to be different. We saw this form of harassment and discrimination with the young female student from Massachusetts who committed suicide due to constant group intimidation. As immoral as isolated and group discrimination are, we believe that the notion of indirect institutionalized discrimination is what undergirds both forms of intolerance. Educators and school officials have to take responsibility for their culpability in the damage to the lives of students as a result of bullying and harassment. We appeal to educators and school leaders to effectively address these issues within their school. And we believe that a multicultural educational approach is a comprehensive method for dealing with such issues.

Here, we offered the school climate perspective, the theoretical perspective, and the educational perspective of multicultural education as a way in which educators and school leaders can begin to address student bullying. If educators and school leaders can recognize the devastating impact that indirect institutionalized discrimination has on their school culture, it is a major win for all involved. And perhaps we will begin to witness fewer fights among student as well as a dramatic decrease in students taking their own lives. Bullying isn't a rite of passage, nor does it give credence to the axiom "Boys will be boys." When harassment and discrimination are allowed to flourish as a part of the school culture, it is a negative reflection on the adults who have been charged with the responsibility of engaging in an ethic of care for all students regardless of their station in life.

3

Taboo Dating in the 21st Century at Payton High School

Case Study

Fred Jones recently became the principal at Payton High School, the only high school in Payton, a small but growing town in the southeastern United States. Fred has lived in this community nearly all his life and was a great student/athlete at Payton High some 20 years ago. It has been Fred's dream to become principal of Payton since he was a young boy. There was something about being the principal of Payton High that earned the respect of the Payton residents. The principals of Payton High School have always been treated with a certain amount of dignity. As one walks in the school building and proceeds past the office to the left, all of the principals' portraits are visible. These portraits do not take up a lot of wall space because, in the school's 100 years, only eight principals have led the Rebels to academic excellence. It is the school's academic reputation that has allowed the principals to be so highly regarded in the community.

School Leadership in a Diverse Society, pages 43–54
Copyright © 2014 by Information Age Publishing
All rights of reproduction in any form reserved.

Payton High School has been able to perform well academically and socially because each principal was able to provide the proper leadership in relation to the cultural dynamics of the community and school. Providing the proper leadership as it related to the cultural dynamics was somewhat effortless because Payton had historically been a small homogenous town. Everyone in the community understood the dominant macroculture that existed, and nearly all practiced the same rituals and lived by the same norms and standards. It was a community where everyone kind of knew everyone, and people came together to celebrate their heritage. It was a good community.

By the time Fred became the principal of Payton High School, many things had changed since he had walked its halls as a student. The school's student body had grown to 700. The Payton community was no longer homogenous. As a result of the small influx of companies from other geographical areas in the country, the Payton community had become more culturally and socially diverse. Consequently, the new diversity that Payton was experiencing brought with it different cultures and values to the small town. Nevertheless, despite these demographic changes, the culture that existed 30 years ago still remained the dominant culture in the community. And because of the heterogeneous environment that had begun to develop, the high school encountered a few minor problems, but it still maintained its reputation of academic excellence.

One major problem that Payton began to encounter was the "taboo" issue of same-sex dating. In large part, the citizens of Payton had not given the subject a second thought because Payton had always been a community that upheld the most traditional values, especially when it came to issues relating to one's sexuality. Traditionally, same-sex dating certainly would have been condemned by the Payton community had the issue come up. But that was then—this is now. The people and policymakers of this nation and its states are talking publicly about same-sex marriages; they are in the news. And now there are some same-sex couples who want to attend prom.

Parents' Perspective

This was an issue Fred had to deal with immediately. There were a number of parents calling Fred's office complaining about same-sex dating among the students at Payton High School. Fred knew that the culture of Payton was not conducive to this type of behavior. The situation had become so tense that several of the community members asked Fred to ban same-sex couples from attending the prom and from any interaction during school hours. Their rationale: this behavior was damaging to the school's culture and causing irreversible damage to the rest of the student body.

Jennifer, a junior at Payton, and her mother were out shopping over the weekend and just happened to see one of Jennifer's classmates. He was a new student who had moved from the Northeast to the town of Payton. As Jennifer and her mother passed Rick, the new student, she exchanged greetings with him. Naturally, Jennifer's mother, a concerned parent, asked Jennifer who the young man was. Jennifer told her mother that he was a new student at the high school. However, Jennifer also added something else. She told her mother that she overheard other students discussing how they were going to beat him up on prom night. This led her mother to inquire as to why the other students would do such a thing.

Jennifer responded, "Well, I am not really sure, but I think it has something to do with who he is."

In a very skeptical voice, Jennifer's mother asked, "Who is he?"

Jennifer responded by saying, "Mother, I would rather not say . . . it's not a big deal." But Jennifer's mother continued to press as to why the other students would want to harm their classmate.

"Jennifer, I want to know why the other students are going to beat up Rick, and I want you to tell me right now!" At this point Jennifer told her mother that there was speculation that Rick was gay and he was "seeing" Bobby, another student at Payton High School. In a state of disbelief, Jennifer's mother indicated in a very stunned voice, "Are you sure . . . I mean . . . do Bobby's parents know about this . . . what about the principal . . . does he know?"

Jennifer, in a very irritated voice stated, "Does who know what, mother . . . I mean what is the big deal? They are not the only gay or lesbian couple at school."

The next morning, Fred received a phone call from Jennifer's mother. She asked Fred if he was aware of the situation in his school. Fred asked the parent to be more specific because, at that point, he was not aware of any major problem that was taking place in the school.

Jennifer's mother responded, "Mr. Jones, I think that you should know that you have students in your school who are doing some immoral things . . . I mean you have gay and lesbian students in your school. My daughter and I were in the mall yesterday, and we saw the new student . . . I think his name is Rick. Do you know who my daughter told me that he is dating?" Before Fred could respond, the mother told him whom Rick was reportedly dating. Fred was stunned but told the parent that he did not consider this issue a major problem and that perhaps this was something that the parents would have to work out themselves. In a state of disbelief, Jennifer's mother also informed Fred that there were some students who were planning on beating up Rick and Bobby at the prom. She told Fred that he should start taking this issue seriously before someone gets hurt.

With this unexpected phone call, Fred began to rearrange his schedule quickly. The very thought that violence could occur at the school prom or at any other time at his school sent his day into disarray. To make matters worse, Jennifer's mother was not the only parent who called. Other parents called Fred the same day with the same message. The message was that some students at Payton High are committing sinful acts. Fred was asked the same question over and over: "What was he going to do about the same-sex couples who were planning on attending the prom?"

Students' Perspective

Throughout the week, the situation became more intense. Many of the students began to find out that there was controversy surrounding some of their classmates and the school prom. Jennifer, ashamed of her mother, told some of the students what her mother had done. Jennifer was a mature and intelligent young lady who had embraced diversity and cultural/social issues throughout most of her school years. As the days proceeded, the lines were drawn. Many students argued in the halls on the issue of same-sex dating. Every student in the school seemed to have an opinion about gay and lesbian couples.

Some of the suspected gay and lesbian couples were heard saying, "We are not hurting anyone; why is this a big deal?" One couple even went to Mr. Jones and asked him not to implement a rule banning same-sex couples at the prom because they felt strongly in what they were doing. Just as there were students like Jennifer and more of her friends who thought that people should be able to date or take to the prom anyone of their choice, there were also those students who felt that same-sex dating should not be allowed at prom or in the school. One of the young men who felt so adamantly about banning same-sex couples was Marty; he had discovered that Bobby, one of his closest friends was gay. On at least one occasion, Marty stated rather vocally to Rick and Bobby in the cafeteria, "I never thought that I would have a friend who was gay . . . both of you make me sick." The altercation did not last long. Bobby and Rick only stared back, and a teacher stepped in to defuse the conversation before it could escalate into any physical violence. Marty did not want to be associated with a friend who was gay and later expressed his concern to school officials for Bobby's safety at the prom.

Teachers' Perspective

Fred had heard about the cafeteria confrontation, and he had witnessed a few of the hallway conversations. The situation that was taking place in Payton High School and the Payton community had begun to worry him. In the following days, Fred did an inquiry by observing the school's culture and looking for any signs that an altercation might indeed take place at school or at the prom. On Thursday afternoon, one of the math teachers, Ms. Harper, approached Fred and asked him what was he going to do about the situation. Fred, of course, had a strong idea of what Ms. Harper was referring to but still asked her for specifics. Ms. Harper responded, "Fred, I am not trying to tell you how to operate the school, but there is a crisis brewing if these gay and lesbian couples are allowed to attend the prom. Some students have told me that they have heard that there was going to be major trouble if same-sex couples are allowed to attend. I have asked who is planning this sort of activity but can't find out. And Fred, I am not sure if I want to find out…we do not need this type of stuff going on around here…Fred, if I were you, I would seriously think of a way to stop these couples from attending the prom."After hearing Ms. Harper's comments, Fred was in disbelief. He told the math teacher that he would look into the matter and that he was taking it seriously.

The next morning, Fred came to school even more disheartened. He was beginning to feel the pressure of being an administrator at a school that had so much tradition, and one that meant so much to him. He decided to get the advice of one of his old classmates, Joe Riley, Payton High's agriculture teacher. Fred and Joe had been friends ever since they were in elementary school together. They attended high school together and kept in touch while they were in college. Fred had even tried to get Joe to leave the state with him so they could attend the same school, but Joe had become engaged to his high school sweetheart and decided to stay near the Payton community and attend the University of Mannesville. Nearly everyone in the Payton community, including Fred, knew and respected Joe Riley. Riley had one of the largest construction companies in the county but still taught school. Fred respected that he still had the will and desire to teach and make a difference in the lives of Payton's children.

Fred called Joe into the office early Friday morning and asked him what he thought about the situation. Joe knew what Fred was talking about and could also see that the situation was taking its toll on Fred and the rest of the school. Joe told Fred that nearly everyone who was coming into his company's office had something to say about this situation. He said that 99.9% were against it. Joe also responded, "Fred, I have to tell you that the major players in the city and county are not for this type of behavior at school or a prom. And they feel very strongly about this issue. I can't tell you what to do . . . but I will keep my ears open and find out anything you want me to. I have also heard the talk that there will be violence if the couples are allowed to attend the prom." Fred told Joe that he had heard the same thing and wanted to make another inquiry into the possibility that some students might start trouble at the prom. But Fred told Joe that his main priority was protecting everyone at school and the prom, including same-sex couples.

A Board Member's Perspective

To make matters worse, the parents and community leaders were not the only ones who were calling on Fred to ban same-sex couples at the school and the prom. On Friday afternoon, with the prom now only 3 weeks away, Mike Porter, a board member, stopped by Fred's office. He wanted to discuss the situation brewing in the school. Porter said that the board was fully prepared to support Fred's decision, and Fred did not have to worry about any reprisal from the board. It was the best news Fred had heard all day. Fred now knew he could stop worrying about his job security for making a decision the community did not favor.

After Fred and Mike discussed the situation for a couple of minutes, Mike asked Fred if he would like to get a beer and watch the NCAA basketball tournament. Fred had known this particular board member for over 20 years. Therefore, Fred was able to have a closer relationship with at least one of his board members than most principals had. While watching the game, Fred once again expressed his gratitude to Porter and the board for showing their support for him. Fred admitted that he had been struggling with the issue all this week and did not know precisely how to handle it. Porter told Fred that he could stop worrying about the situation and enjoy the game. Porter stated, "Everyone knows that we are not going to let gays and lesbians attend the prom. This is something that the community would not tolerate. The community leaders will not stand for it. Let Massachusetts and California deal with it." Mr. Porter went on to commend Fred on how he had handled the situation. Porter conveyed to Fred that he showed signs of a great leader, and everyone in the school district was proud that he was principal of Payton. Porter also said that the board made a good decision by hiring a "hometown boy" and not an outsider. He stated, "Lord knows how this situation might have turned out if we had not hired a Payton grad; all of the couples at the prom might have been gays or either lesbians. But no sir . . . no sir . . . thank God we hired someone who knows the culture of our community."

Porter went on to tell Fred that he must be very careful in how he dissuades the same-sex couples from attending prom because he did not want things to get out of hand. He said, "It reminds me of a book that I read many years ago while I was in college. The author of the book, Machiavelli, found that a leader should be a "fox when it comes to suspecting a trap and a lion when it comes to making the wolves turn tail." You've done a great job, Fred. Hell, some in the community actually thought that you were going to allow these same-sex couples to attend prom." Nevertheless, Porter commended Fred again on how he handled the situation. He told Fred that the board and the superintendent would get back in contact with him so they could figure out a way to make this issue go away peacefully.

Fred went to bed that night devastated by what he had heard from Mr. Porter. He could not believe that Porter had displayed these beliefs as a board member and public servant. He felt like a ton of bricks had been placed on his back. Fred had even started to question whether the couples should be permitted to attend. But Fred constantly reflected back on his experiences outside the Payton community. While away at college, Fred was able to experience diversity across lines of race, gender, and sexual orientation, while most people in his community could only imagine that type of diversity. This experience gave Fred the foundation to appreciate cultural and social heterogeneity. However, Fred's revelations while in college were also a source of great inner conflict. While realizing the great personal value of respecting differences, Fred also reflected on the norms and attitudes of his hometown. The perspectives held in his community were very different from those experienced in college; the two places seemed very distant, both geographically and philosophically, to Fred at that moment. But he also knew that there were legal issues that also must be dealt with concerning students' freedom of expression and equal protection.

With expression rights, there is a freedom to associate; and simply being homosexual is certainly not illegal. And parallel to the current national dialogue on same-sex marriages, would a school policy that is applied against homosexual couples and not heterosexual couples be illegal? What if student safety were the stated justification for the policy? Would that not be enough to justify a limit on speech and conduct? With all of these thoughts swimming in his head, Fred also began to question whether this issue would affect his job at Payton.

Fred's Proposed Solution: The Meeting at the Diner

The next morning, Fred thought of an idea on how to handle the situation. He immediately called Mr. Porter and the superintendent, Kenneth Wilson, and asked them both to meet him at the local diner for lunch. Wilson and Porter agreed to meet. At the diner, Fred told Porter and Wilson that he was not going to ban same-sex couples from attending the prom. This came as a complete surprise. Porter and Wilson asked Fred what he was thinking and reiterated that the community would not stand for same-sex couples at the prom. Fred told both men that it was a decision that should be left up to parents. Fred said, "If the parents do not want their children to attend the prom with someone of the same sex, then the parents get to make that decision." Fred told the superintendent and the board member that this was the best solution and that he thought the proposal would go over well since all three men were aware that most of the parents in Payton were totally against this type of behavior.

Nevertheless, Porter indicated, "Fred, I don't like this idea one bit because most of the parents I've talked to have stated that they want the school to make the statement too. And they do not want their kids exposed to this type behavior. What is preventing these gay and lesbian students from coming to the prom even after their parents have forbidden them to? Fred, I don't like it. You need to come up with another solution. Maybe a ban on the couples because of safety reasons or something. And you do know that some of our boys are planning on causing trouble for this Rick character and Bobby. I am totally shocked at Bobby." After a quick pause, Porter continued, "And I've already heard the First Amendment argument that the gays and lesbians are entitled to "their rights." I know about that recent sodomy case from the Supreme Court. But frankly, we can't give these students free reign. Who cares about their rights! What happens if we let them go and there's a riot at the prom?"

Fred was now in disarray because he had felt confident that Mr. Porter would accept this solution. Wilson expressed concern over the board and central office putting its stamp of approval on such conduct: "This is a school-sponsored event. This has never been the sort of value system Payton has adopted. We aren't ready to start now." Subsequently, Porter asked Wilson if he were ready to lose his job over such nonsense. In this county, the superintendent is elected into office. Porter told Wilson that a policy of supporting same-sex couples at the prom could cost him reelection and lead other board members to defeat.

Fred became more disheartened at the comments being made by Porter and Wilson. But Fred held firm and reiterated that he felt uncomfortable banning these kids from the prom, arguing that to do so would be unethical and probably illegal. It was at this point that Porter became outraged at Fred's comments and said "You mean to sit there and tell me that you would be defiant against our wishes and allow these gays and lesbians to attend the prom? Fred, our community does not want this type of behavior at the prom. . . . nor in the halls of our schools. We will not tolerate it; I have to answer to the community. Now, I suggest that you think this thing through clearly."

Fred told Mr. Porter that he had indeed thought it through clearly, and he thought he was making the right decision.

Conclusion

Fred has now been delivered his first major dilemma as principal. He has come to realize that the culture of the community is a powerful apparatus that can be used for or against him. One wrong decision could ruin his dreams of being the next admired principal of Payton High School. It could actually cost him the job. To make matters worse, Fred had recently purchased a $200,000 house. This was not a bad decision because the average tenure of a principal at Payton High is over 10 years. It is a job that a person could have for as long as he or she wanted, but apparently the "right" decisions had to be made.

If he bans same-sex dating, is he violating the First Amendment freedom of speech and association rights of teenagers? Does the Fourteenth Amendment, which guarantees equal protection under the law, prevent a policy that categorizes people on the basis of their sexual orientation, even if the policy is motivated by safety? Is he unethically invading the personal lives of others? Is he doing so just to protect his job? If he allows same-sex dating, is he opening the school to the "rumbles" of *West Side Story* times ten? Of course, there are potential liability issues if foreseeable fights occur without school action. But if Fred warns the students in advance to obey the code, will they rebel and make matters worse? If he refrains from such a warning and the fights occur, liability lawsuits are sure to follow. What about the enforcement of the school's code of conduct on harassment and fighting? Is a policy statement on same-sex dating even within the jurisdiction of school leadership?

Fred knows that a ban on same-sex dating goes against what he personally stands for in life. As far as he is concerned, unless they directly affect the operation of the school and the welfare of the kids, dating decisions made by teenagers belong to the parents and teens themselves. However, there are many in the community who feel that such behavior is causing major disruptions in the school, which brings to the forefront the question of how we balance issues concerning students' freedom of expression and liabilities and damages that may occur as a result. In essence, Fred, as a school administrator, is not an opponent of or advocate for same-sex dating. Nevertheless, his decision could end up being a burning bale of hay left unattended in the middle of the night.

Teaching Notes

Within the context of same-sex dating at a high school prom in a traditional, but now culturally and socially diverse community, the principal (Fred) must address legal, ethical, and policymaking issues. The resolution of these issues could dictate the most appropriate course of action. To leave one of these issues out of the mix could erase Fred's good work at the school and good standing in the community.

Legal Issues

1. Is it a violation of the students' free speech/expression rights for the principal to adopt a policy that forbids same-sex couples at the high school prom? To defend such a restriction, can administrators rely on the fact that the prom is school-sponsored?
2. Is a potential conflict at the dance enough to permit the restriction on same-sex couples at the prom? Or does Fred have to wait until after a "riot" to step in?
3. Will the school be subject to successful liability lawsuits should a fight break out at the prom?
4. How much weight should be placed on the community's wishes versus students' right of freedom of speech and equal protection?
5. How might the following cases guide Fred in his decision making concerning the allowing or banning of same-sex couples at the prom? *Fricke v. Lynch,* 491 U.S. 381 (1980); *Tinker v. Des Moines Independent Community School District,* 393 U.S. 503 (1969); *Bethel School District No. 403 v. Fraser,* 478 U.S. 675 (1986); and *Harper v. Edgewood Board of Education,* 655 F. Supp. 1353 (S.D. Ohio 1987).
6. See also the following cases concerning student harassment and equal protection: *Davis v. Monroe County Board of Education,* 526 U.S. 629 (1999); *Nabozny v. Podlesny,* 92 F.3d 446 (7th Cir. 1996); and *Flores v. Morgan Hill Unified School District,* 324 F.3d 1130 (9th Cir. 2003).

Ethical Issues

1. Fred must grapple with the divergent values and beliefs of each of the affected parties. Therefore, to what extent should Fred's

decision be grounded in the rights of the individuals as opposed to the good of the entire organization?

2. Obviously, Fred must care for the students. But to what degree should he grapple with the possible conflict between his personal views and his professional responsibilities?

3. Is Fred acting within ethical bounds if he bases his decisions, in part, on his own personal values and/or personal employment situation? What if those values are affected by Porter's insinuation that Fred's job may hinge on the decisions made in this matter?

Policymaking Issues

1. Perhaps the most outstanding policymaking issue here is whether Fred should involve all of the competing players and their interests

2. What roles should the superintendent and Board of Education play here? Would Fred be better off if the board simply drafted a policy for the whole district to follow?

3. Is Fred expected to defer to the wishes of the administrators and policymakers above him? Or has he been given the green light to make the decision as he sees fit?

4. What about the stakeholders within his own building? How much should the teachers, staff, students, and parents be involved?

5. What decisions can be made now, without new policy statements on the specifics of same-sex dating? What guidance does current policy offer?

6. If the larger goal is education in an increasingly diverse democratic society, is Fred necessarily better off by giving students and parents a voice in school policy? What are the advantages and disadvantages?

This chapter was reprinted from McCray, C. R., Pauken, P., & Beachum, F. D. (2004). Taboo dating in the 21st century at Payton High School. *Journal of Cases in Educational Leadership,* 7(3), 12–21.

SECTION **II**

4

The Role of Principals as Bridge Builders

A majority of school principals have become inundated with school reform measures that require technocratic skillsets and can all but dis-
miss the humanistic and soft skills that are just as important in creating a
successful school climate and culture (Hersey et al., 1996). Thus, what we
are proposing here in this chapter is a conflation of those technocratic and
humanistic skillsets for better collaboration between school leaders and
their community stakeholders. We propose that such a marriage will produce more dedication, commitment, and trust among school leaders with
students and members of their respective communities. It is important for
us to address how this relationship might look in action. Unfortunately, this
kind of scholarship is often appreciated in theory but lacks cogent practice.
Ergo, the support of such collaborative efforts should be well grounded
in appropriate conceptual frameworks and at the same time be palpable
enough to inform the daily work that goes on in schools and communities.

It is with these considerations that we offer the following suggestions
for school leaders looking to form stronger relationships with the students
and communities: (a) *principals should become more reflective of the communities*

School Leadership in a Diverse Society, pages 57–75
Copyright © 2014 by Information Age Publishing
All rights of reproduction in any form reserved.

they are serving; (b) *establish community networks to ascertain community percep-tions and perspectives;* (c) *cultivate equity audits skillsets;* (d) *become proactive in engaging the community;* and (e) *become risk takers and innovators in meeting the needs of the students and community.* Of course, these five suggestions are not exhaustive when it comes to principals' endeavors in building bridges with their communities, but they will provide some guidance for schools leaders as they continue to seek out better ways to collaborate with parents and other community members. In this chapter, we intend to cover each one of these processes in-depth with the hope of stimulating discussions that will help our schools become more community centered in their practice.

Being Reflective in Serving the Community

Too often, school administrators take on the leadership position within the school without giving much consideration to community needs. Research-ers (Berliner, 2006; Miller, Brown, & Hopson, 2011) have opined that this is a critical mistake by those who have a desire to become effective leaders. In order for school leaders to become reflective agents with regard to the communities they serve, they must be cognizant of the need to *critique* what is going on within their schools as well as within the community (Berliner, 2006; Starratt 2004). School leaders must also be able to institute a sense of *care* within their practice. In many instances, school administrators take on leadership positions in communities where there are cultural mismatches between their own cultural background and the background of their stake-holders (i.e., parents and students) (Beachum & McCray, 2011; McCray et al., 2004;). We believe that it is extremely disingenuous for school leaders to take on these roles without giving serious thought to how their cultur-al backgrounds might adversely impact their student population, who in many instances do not share the same outlooks (Haberman, 2005). Finally, once school administrators have critiqued the situation of the community and made strides to create an ethic of care as it relates to those individuals within their communities, these leaders need to have the courage to imple-ment a form of justice that ensures all students receive an equitable educa-tion as a result of a school culture and climate that empowers everyone.

As we just stated, Starratt's (2004) *ethic of critique* has a place in the re-flection process for school leaders. Starratt has found that a cogent form of critique entails the notion of school leaders recognizing that societies have generally consisted of those who have struggled for control of resources. According to Starratt (1991),

The point of . . . [this] critical stance is to uncover which group has the advantage over the other, how things got to be the way they are, and to expose how situations are structured and language is used so as to maintain the legitimacy of social arrangement. (p. 189)

Harris (2011) illustrates this point just as succinctly, opining that "social reproduction theorists argue that schools maintain existing patterns of inequality because they are structured to reproduce the current social order." (p. 9) Harris attributes this ideological perspective to Bowles and Gintis' (1976) and Bourdieu and Passeron's (1977) notion of reproduction of social class inequality. According to Harris (2011), many schools have in essence become status quo organizations designed to reproduce a cycle of socialization (Barta, 1996) in which students continue to find themselves in the positions from which they originally started.

McCray and Beachum (2006) have proffered that school leaders who are serious about subscribing to the ethic of critique might considered asking a series of questions such as, Who defines? Who controls? and Who is benefiting by such arrangement? McCray and Beachum went on to indicate that the ethic of critique is an excellent way for school administrators to begin to problematize community-related issues in the spirit of building bridges. And from an urban context, such an ethic of critique is critical. It recognizes the dire situation that many urban communities have to encounter and how these issues ultimately impact the school. Because of the strong intersection of school- and community-related issues, school leaders can ill afford to ignore critical issues within the community and how in many instances it perpetuates inequality (Wilson, 2009). So, what type of inquiry should school leaders be engaging in that meets the spirit of Starratt's (2004) ethic of critique? The potential answer to this question is broached in one of our classes called Strategic Thinking and Planning. Each time this class is taught, students, as well as school leaders at the building level and district level, are asked to consider thinking strategically at the megalevel (Kaufman, 1995). We find that many of our urban students come to the class with the best of intentions of solving issues related to the academic achievement gap, high attrition rate of their students as well as their teachers, and various other problems plaguing their schools. However, many of the students in the strategic thinking class very seldom have admitted to thinking and planning at a megalevel. The megalevel requires school leaders to engage in those tough questions dealing with community-related issues and to address the school's role in helping ameliorate conditions that have proven to be detrimental to the community. Kaufman found that the underpinnings of megalevel planning is committing to a vision and long-term goals that exist outside of the school.

Such visions and long-term goals have to be altruistic and earnest with regard to the current situation of the community the leader has chosen become a part of. For instance, much has been written about the problems plaguing the inner city. The issues are very pronounced in academic literature, newspapers, and among educators and the general public. Scholars (R. R. Banks, 2011; Cosby & Poasiant, 2007; Harris, 2011) have found that Black males have some of the highest unemployment rates in country. A substantial number of Black males today find themselves underemployed, unemployed, as well as revolving through the penal system (R. R. Banks, 2011). According to Day-Vines and Day-Hairston (2005), "52% of African American males who departed prematurely from school had prison records by their 30s." And current projections indicate that 32% of Black males are likely to serve prison terms (Day-Vines & Day-Hairston, 2005).

Thus, it is a critical mistake for school leaders to acquiesce to the political pseudo-educational policies delivered to them by plutocrats, which call for only technocratic skills dealing with literacy and numeracy testing at the expense of understanding major issues that are plaguing many communities. We proffer that by school leaders engaging the community with regard to social inequality and coming up with long-term goals and visions at the megalevel will only enhance the educative process for all students. But we have to point out a critical obstacle to school leaders engaging in an ethic of critique at a megalevel. When there is not a cognitive dissonance to what is going on at the megalevel, it is very problematic to conduct an earnest critique. In other words, school leaders must find the aforementioned current plight of Black males, for example, at the megalevel discomforting and unsettling in order for an ethic of critique at the megalevel to come to fruition.

In order for the critique that school administrators conduct on the issues and problems within the community to be genuine, it needs to be undergirded by an ethic of care. According to McCray and Beachum (2006), "The ethic of care is a principle that examines the quality of relationships or interactions between individuals" (p. 5). Starratt (1991) has found that "such an ethic does not demand a relationship of intimacy; rather, it postulates a level of caring that honors the dignity of each person and desires to see that that a person enjoys a fully human life." (p. 196) Adding to this perspective, McCray and Beachum (2006) opined that "When an individual has decided that he or she will care for another individual, a certain amount of growth and development should be derived from the relationship" (p. 5). Likewise, Mayeroff (1971) has found that the essence of a caring relationship is the ability to cultivate growth in another individual. And the underpinnings of cultivating growth in another individual are the ability to have patience and the stamina to persist in difficult situations (Mayeroff, 1971).

The ethic of care has to be a part of any school leaders' reflection process. When school leaders engage in serious reflections, they begin to determine if there has been growth among community stakeholders. School leaders ask themselves how they have contributed to the growth of the community as a whole. It is not enough, as we indicated earlier, for school leaders to simply focus on literacy and numeracy, especially when school administrators have a deficit mindset toward their school's community. This deficit mindset occurs because of the cultural disconnect between the community where the school is located and the school leader's own cultural values. Alas, many educators and school leaders do not attempt to reconcile these mismatches in a positive and cohesive manner. Instead, they acquiesce to deficit thinking, wherein their ideological perspective ends up doing more harm than good. Deficit thinking is when educators and school leaders perceive that the student's culture is in complete need of amelioration due to the student's lack of cultural and social capital.

Freire (1998) indicates that instead of educators and school leaders focusing on the deficits of their students, they must be cognizant of their own shortcomings. Freire refers to the notion of people interrogating and critiquing their own ideological certitude and perspective as a sense of "unfinishedness." The notion of unfinishedness is something that school leaders and educators have to be cognizant of when reflecting on an ethic of care. Dantley et al. (2008) stated that the concept of unfinishedness "is our immersion into the consciousness of our incompleteness that motivates searching and inquiry." They went on to indicate the following concerning Freire's notion of unfinishedness:

> Our unfinishedness leads us to an understanding of the world, also to the creation of strategies to transform and resist those traditional forms and rituals that perpetuate undemocratic and marginalizing practices in schools. If we find ourselves believing that our particular position on social justice is finished, we therefore leave ourselves in an untenable space where neither further learning nor broadening of our perspectives is possible.

We believe that Starratt's (2004) ethic of care is undergirded by Freire's (1998) notion of unfinishedness, especially when it comes to educators and school leaders reflecting on their interaction with the community. It is almost inconceivable to see how one subscribes to an ethic of care without recognizing the need for further development. Without an understanding of our own biases and prejudices and continuing the struggle to recognize our limitations, we do a disservice to an ethics of care, and the caring ends up being inauthentic at best.

Starratt's (2004) ethical framework calls on school leaders to unearth inequalities by critiquing policies and procedures. It also asks those in charge of schools to become more cognizant of what it means to genuinely care for another, especially those for whom school leaders are charged with the mission of providing growth and development. Therefore, a critical aspect of being reflective while serving the community is also undergirded by the marriage of praxis and an ethic of justice. Here, we intimate that the underpinning of an ethic of justice is school leaders' ability to parlay their sense of critique and care into a cogent form of praxis that allows all students to excel.

"An ethic of justice addresses the issue of governance and fairness," according to McCray and Beachum (2006, p. 3). Walker and Snarey (2004) have found that "justice means liberating others from injustice and orientating oneself away from biases and partial passions and towards universal ethical principles" (p. 4). While we can certainly appreciate Walker and Snarey's viewpoint concerning orienting oneself toward justice and righteousness and away from "biases and partial passions," we would like to offer an alternative measure with regard to the act of liberating. To us, the act of liberating signifies the perspective that certain groups of people are not strong, intelligent, or capable enough to do for themselves. When we think of liberating, images of the Allied troops storming Normandy on D-Day to rescue France and all of Europe come to mind. Now, we certainly recognize that there comes a time when individuals, through no fault of their own, need some assistance and even liberating. During slavery, African Americans certainly needed liberating from slave holders. And President Lincoln, along with the Northern Army, was a godsend to many individuals who were held in bondage. Likewise, during World War II, the Allied army played a critical role in helping to save Europe from calamity. Although liberators have their place, we think it is a huge mistake for educators to see themselves at liberators. In fact, we think this is almost tantamount to educational malpractice.

Thus, if we believe it is educational malpractice for educators and educational leaders to view themselves as liberators, then what role should educators have when it comes to establishing a relationship with the community and subscribing to an ethic of justice? When it comes to justice in the United States and rethinking the term "liberator" among educators and school leaders, we believe that it is the Civil Right Movement that ultimately provides us with an example of how to rethink that term. Most scholars of history would agree that a liberator was nowhere to be found during the

Civil Rights Movement. But the Civil Rights Movement did have some dynamic leaders as well as some loyal foot soldiers. It is well documented how the notion of *group solidarity* resonated with many African Americans in the 1960s. Such solidarity allowed Blacks to "stick together" and form a cohesive unit in order to achieve equality in the United States. And not only did group solidarity become more prevalent among African Americans during this time, but the Civil Rights Movement also began to witness an insurgency taking shape when individuals from outside the solidarity movement (i.e., liberal Whites, Jewish people, the news media, high profile entertainers, etc.) started to join the struggle for Blacks securing equal rights.

An insurgency takes place when individuals who are not directly related to the struggles of a marginalized group immerse themselves in the struggle (McCray, 2008). McCray (2008) opined that "the insurgency [during the Civil Rights Movement] was carried out only when liberal and progressive Whites with resources...[joined the movement] in order to help change structural powers" (p. 148). As was pointed out, many school administrators are not from the same communities where the schools they are leading are situated. Thus, it is somewhat problematic and maybe even unrealistic for school leaders to have a sense of group solidarity with individuals from their school's community, since group solidarity is usually predicated on the notion that people with similar characteristics struggling for justice is requisite.

A plethora of communities in urban areas are in dire straits as they continue the fight for justice (i.e., better quality of education, more jobs in the community, a reduction of students dropping out of school, etc.). Ergo, in many instances, they are in desperate need of earnest partners to help facilitate and promote community development. And we would certainly argue that school leaders are not able to fulfill such a role in an oblique space, that is, having limited or inauthentic contact with the school's community. In order for an ethic of justice to register high on school leaders' epistemological frame of reference, they must see themselves as insurgents with their respective communities, with the realization they might not share similar characteristics of the communities in which they work (Haberman, 2005) but are committed to help assuage the heavy burden such communities are facing. We believe this commitment is at the epicenter of Starratt's (2004) ethics of justice.

Establish Community Networks to Ascertain Community Perspectives and Perceptions

It is imperative for school leaders to cultivate networks within the community to ensure that those stakeholders who can provide vital support to the school's mission are kept abreast of the direction of the school. We mentioned the insurgency model as a way that school leaders can form bonds with their communities in order to commit themselves to an *ethic of justice.* Educators and school officials are often oblivious to the role community members and community leaders can play in the enhancement of the school's culture and its mission. Because school leaders and educators often overlook those vital resources within the community, a contentious relationship emerges between school administrators and their community stakeholders.

Even though the U.S. Constitution declares that there is a separation between church and state, we believe that it is a mistake for school leaders to not take advantage of religious institutions within the community that are readily available to assist in the process of educating its citizenry. McCray et al. (2010) elucidated a framework for school leaders forming networks with religious institutions for the betterment of all involved. The underpinnings of such a framework intersect with the notion of the insurgency model. Even though school administrators might not share the same religious beliefs or religious affiliation as the stakeholders in the community, educators and school leaders must be fearless in their efforts to connect with such faith-based institutions.

McCray et al. (2007) have found in their study that many school principals who lead schools in which there is a heavy concentration of people of color in the community are not of the same ethnic background. Certainly, it would be a mistake on our part to put forth a supposition that school principals have to be of the same ethnic background as the communities in which they work. Nevertheless, in many instances, there does seem to be a cultural and social disconnect between school administrators and those they are serving in the community. Thus, when it comes to connecting with communities of color, school administrators must see the relevance of connecting with religious institutions to propagate their message, listen attentively, and give voice to those with an interest in student success. For school leaders who work in heavily populated communities of color, the infrastructure is already in place to help provide assistance. For example, "Historically, the Black church has been an institutional stronghold in the Black community and has thereby sustained a cultural ethos that has enabled African Americans to combat racial prejudice and hostility for generations," according to McCray et al. (2010).

In earlier chapters, we referred to the notion of culturally relevant leadership wherein we emphasized liberatory consciousness, pluralistic insight, and reflexive practice as the underpinnings of such leadership. When formulating networks with faith-based institutions, school leaders might find culturally relevant leadership practices helpful as they attempt to navigate different cultural terrains. Here, liberatory consciousness requires school leaders to become aware of those networking opportunities that exist within their communities. Oftentimes, school leaders are not aware of such opportunities for a number of reasons. We believe that one of the main reasons is school leaders not being cognizant of the plethora of opportunities that exist within communities that are heavily populated with people of color. Thus, many religious institutions can provide crucial historical memory and historical context, such as information about the local community, demographic changes, and local people of interest. This information is valuable for those leaders who want to awaken their consciousness toward those whom they are serving. We believe that it is a mistake as well as educational malpractice for school leaders to attempt to formulate and implement policies and decisions within his or her school without allowing their consciousness to be awakened.

Pluralistic insight is also critical when forming networks in the community. School leaders can have their liberatoy consciousness awakened with regard to contextualizing their school's community, but if they are unwilling to cultivate the community's voice within their school's mission, policy initiatives, and overall direction, such conscious awakening results in anemic decision making. It is disingenuous at best for school leaders to gain a better understanding of the community of their school without acknowledging the right of those in the community to have a greater voice. Once again, religious institutions have a role here by propagating the values and mores that are entrenched in the community and by being an interlocutor or advocate for those values. Without the conflation of school leader's pluralistic insight and the advocacy that such religious institutions can provide, there is the possibility that school administrators can regress in their praxis in ensuring that all students have the opportunity to achieve their goals.

McCray et al. (2004) published a case in the *Journal of Cases in Educational Leadership* wherein they challenged school administrators to take up the mantle of culturally relevant leadership. This challenge was undergirded by the notion of same-sex students attending the prom with overwhelming opposition from community leaders. In essence, the majority of the community members were opposed to same-sex couples attending the prom together. We broach this particular issue now as a form of a caution to school administrators when cultivating such networking opportunities with faith-based institutions. For example, Reed (2008) found in her research that homophobia is well entrenched in the many Black churches as well as other religious institutions. Although we strongly advocate the need for school leaders to build bridges with religious organizations as part of their networking endeavors, a caveat is warranted when it comes to ideologies that such organization might have as to the disenfranchisement of students due to their religious beliefs and sexual orientation. Thus, reflexive practice is critical in this regard. According to McCray et al. (2010), "Reflective practice views educators (teachers and administrators) as change agents who engage in ongoing praxis (reflection and action) for overall better student outcomes."

Most religious organizations, especially Black churches, have embedded in their mission the need to fight for social justice. This has certainly been the case historically with the Black church, which has been at the vanguard of fighting for civil rights and social justice. During the 60s, the Black church had a very dominant role in ensuring that the Civil Rights Movement was successful. When there was hopelessness, the church helped shed light on the practices of injustice that were widespread in the Deep South. Nevertheless, it is a mistake for school leaders to assume that because religious organizations have been entrenched in battles for social justice that they will automatically support the aforementioned issue of same-sex dating. This is when reflexive practice is critical. School leaders must be willing to engage in fearless speech (Applebaum, 2010) when it comes to ensuring that all students in their building are able to succeed and enjoy their experience in the educative process. The notion of fearless speech entails school leaders engaging religious leaders and other community members on issues that have arisen as a result of the school leaders' liberatory conscious awakening and their pluralistic insight (Applebaum, 2010). Nevertheless, Paulo Freire (1998), in his insightful book, *Pedagogy of Freedom*, warned that to engage in absolute certitude runs the risk of alienating others. Thus, we argue that school leaders must be ambidextrous when working with communities and faith-based institutions. School administrators must be willing to engage the community and religious organization with fearless speech in advocating for all students while not acquiescing to their own certitude. This form of ambidexterity is somewhat difficult, we readily admit. However, it is increasingly becoming a requisite for school leaders who are trying to make a difference in the communities they serve.

Cultivate Action Research and Equity Audit Skillsets

Today, educational leaders are being asked more than ever before to become technocrats within their discipline. We mentioned this briefly in the beginning of this chapter. Technocrats are usually defined as those individuals with a certain amount of technical expertise on a particular issue. In Europe over the past year, we have seen the rise of many technocrats in government's highest positions trying to stabilize their economies (Krugman, 2011). But in his op-ed piece titled, Eurozone Crisis: To Save Europe, Topple the "Technocrats," Krugman argued that societies whose economies are on the verge of collapse should tread cautiously in totally capitulating to the ideology of pseudo-technocrats. The underpinnings of Krugman's argument were simple: in many instances, these countries do not or did not have serious technocrats in charge of the stewardship of the economy. Krugman opined that "real technocrats" ask the hard and difficult questions when trying to ameliorate problems and identify real solutions. Regardless of whether one thinks that the economic problems of today can be solved by heavy spending or a retreat to austerity, Krugman put forth a cogent argument in his *New York Times* op-ed piece that challenged economic technocrats to ask the hard and difficult questions.

In the era of high-stakes testing, increased accountability measures, privatization of K–12 education, and constant changes in educational policies, school leaders are becoming more technocratic by the day. But in the spirit of Paul Krugman's (2011) op-ed piece, are school leaders becoming pseudo-technocrats in an effort to placate outside entities and the increasing pressures that come with the job? To revisit Starratt's (2004) ethics of critique, exactly what does it mean to ask the right questions when it comes to ensuring that all students succeed in the educative process? Skrla, McKenzie, and Scheurich (2009) have acknowledged that "there is currently a large national focus on closing school achievement gaps, but practical information for school leaders to actually use in their efforts to close these gaps is in short supply" (p. 3). We believe that part of this answer is embedded in the notion of school leaders enhancing their skillsets to conduct equity audits and action research within their schools. Such skillsets also increase the rapport between school leaders and their respective stakeholders. Skrla et al. (2009) have found that "the leadership to implement equity audits requires a change agent, and being a successful change agent requires skills and assumptions for working with others" (p. 7).

Equity Audits and Actions Research

Scholars of social justice have found that equity audits are powerful tools that educational leaders can utilized to ensure that their schools are places where all students are given the opportunity to reach their self-actualization. Skrla et al. (2009) have intimated that there are three forms of equity audits that school leaders can utilize to cultivate an equitable school climate and culture: teacher quality equity, programmatic equity, and student achievement equity. The conflation of these three equity audits helps school leaders address inequities at every level in the school.

The teacher quality equity audits are of great importance for any school leader in exhibiting his or her commitment to ensuring the foundation has been laid for student achievement to take place. When it comes to teacher quality equity audits, school leaders should be cognizant of issues surrounding "teacher education, teacher experience, teacher mobility, and teacher certification" (Skrla et al., 2009, p. 7). Equity audits centered around teacher education deal with the number of teachers within the school who hold a bachelor's degree, a master's degree, and a doctorate. In many school districts, teachers are encouraged to go back to school to receive additional professional development or a higher degree. The rationale is simple: teachers who dedicate themselves to becoming lifelong learners are more likely to have better pedagogical skills. And of course, the school leader has a critical role in ensuring that his or her school climate and culture reflect the ideas of lifelong learning and development.

Teaching experience centers on the notion that all students should have access to teachers who have the knowledge, know-how, and capability to deliver cogent instructions. Such knowledge, know-how, and capability usually come with the number of years teachers have had to cultivate such skillsets. Skrla et al. (2009) have found that in many instances, students who are in low-tracked classes usually do not have access to teachers with these increased skills. Those teachers with high instructional skills are routinely placed in higher tracked classes, and teacher quality equity audits require school leaders to be cognizant of the disproportionate number of teachers with more experience as well as advanced degrees who continually teach the "more desirable" students.

The concept of teacher mobility is an issue that warrants a lot of attention from school leaders. Haberman (2005) found that teacher attrition tends to be one of the major problems when dealing with educational equality between urban and suburban districts. According to Haberman, the high attrition rate among urban teachers (i.e., those teacher who choose to leave the teaching profession or their respective school for another school) is untenable if urban schools are expected to close the achievement gap. The high level of teacher attrition among urban teachers was the catalyst for Haberman to advocate that urban school leaders hire more teachers who come from the same community in which the school is located. Haberman also offered the idea that urban school leaders should not hire teachers who are coming straight out of a teacher preparation programs. His rationale for these two thoughts was that teachers who do not come from the community in which they work are not completely invested in the school or the community and are therefore more willing to leave for other appealing opportunities. Haberman also indicated that this seems to be the same situation with young teachers who come straight out of teacher preparation programs. There is a severe cultural disconnect because the majority of these teachers, who are young White women, are usually looking for less threatening positions and opportunities.

A modicum of solace that can be found in the notion of teacher high attrition is the fact that they usually do not leave due to the "bad students"; the departure from the school is usually due to an inadequate school climate and culture as well as a lack of school resources. High teacher attrition is devastating to schools, especially those in urban communities. Thus, school administrators must do everything in their power to help decrease the number of teachers who are leaving their building. This includes doing a better job of hiring as well as cultivating a more conducive school culture and climate that entices teachers to remain in their building.

Finally, when it comes to teacher certification, Skrla, Scheurich, Garcia, and Nolly (2004) elucidated that it is comparable with the concept of teacher education and teacher experience. School leaders should be diligent in ensuring that there is not a disproportionate number of teachers who do not have the proper teaching credentials in the building. Thus, in terms of teaching certification and credentials, school leaders should ensure that a teacher with a reading certification is not teaching mathematics. This form of teaching misplacement only exacerbates the much-publicized issues such as the academic achievement gap.

Skrla et al. (2004) also mentioned the need for school leaders to interrogate programmatic aspects of the school. Here, they encouraged school administrators to take a critical look at their programs dealing with special education, gifted and talented education, bilingual education, and student discipline. Beachum and McCray (2011) have indicated that educators and school leaders should problematize and rupture the trend of overplacing young African American males in special education. According to Beachum and McCray (2011),

> While young Black males consist of 9 percent of the student population, they consist of 20 percent of the number of students enrolled in Special Education classes that offer services to low achievers and mentally impaired. The corollary is that young Black males only represent 4 percent of those individuals in the gifted and talented programs. (p. 77, as cited in J. H. Jackson, 2008)

From the student discipline angle, this is also a critical aspect of programmatic equity audits. McCray and Beachum (2011) found that young Black male students tend to come up on the short end with regard to the high number of suspensions and expulsions they are subject to in the educative process. Remember, in Chapter 1, we mentioned that the *New York Times* reported that Baltimore Public Schools, in the year 2006, handed out 26,000 school suspensions.

Obviously, there is something severely wrong with the aforementioned statistics concerning the placement of African American students in Special Education programs designed for the mentally impaired as opposed to the placement of these student in Gifted and Talented Programs. Likewise, it is also deeply troubling when a school district delivers 26,000 school suspensions within a calendar year. With regard to school suspensions, Peterson (2003) argues that those students who are more subject to school suspension and expulsion are also more likely to drop out of school. Thus, programmatic equity is something that school leaders should definitely be cognizant of because such inequities (i.e., student placement and student discipline) can have a devastating impact on communities.

The third equity audit that Skrla et al. (2009) found to be beneficial to school leaders is the student achievement equity audit. This audit entails school leaders interrogating and critiquing any discrepancies that might exist between groups of students. It has been well documented how there is an academic achievement gap between students of color (i.e., African American and Latino students) and their White counterparts (Harris, 2011). Thus, student achievement equity audits force school leaders to become cognizant of the achievement gap and take effective measures to ameliorate it. Skrla et al. (2009) also found that student achievement equity audits should also focus on student attrition.

In the preceding paragraph, we broached the issues of student suspension and expulsion with regard to programmatic equity audits. We indicated that there was a correlation between high suspensions and expulsion rates and the number of students who drop out of school. So there is definitely an intersection between programmatic equity audits and student achievement equity audits. Programmatic equity audits require school leaders to critically look at the number of students, especially those students within a certain subgroup, who are more likely to be suspended and expelled from school. Likewise, the underpinnings of student achievement equity audits consist of school leaders being aware of the devastating consequences of those suspensions and expulsion vis-à-vis students leaving the educative process altogether (Skrl et al., 2009).

These three equity audits that school leaders have at their disposal are very powerful tools to enhance their skillsets as social justice leaders. Equity audits are also designed to illuminate policies and procedures in which everyone inside as well as outside the organization can be cognizant of where the school is presently situated in terms of mission, ideology, and philosophy, and where it is headed in the future. And it is important to emphasize that school leaders illuminating problems and issues unearthed by equity audits should not be considered a threat to the administrators' educational and leadership abilities in terms of ensuring that all students receive an equitable education. School leaders should welcome the ability (which equity audits provide) to irradiate issues that are impeding the success of all students. According to Skrla et al. (2009), there are seven steps school leaders should employ when using equity audits to ensure the audits are being implemented properly and producing the best results: (a) *Create a committee of relevant stakeholders;* (b) *Present the data to the committee and have everyone graph the data;* (c) *Discuss the meaning of the data, possible use of experts, led by a facilitator;* (d) *Discuss potential solutions, possible use of experts, led by a facilitator;* (e) *Implement solutions;* (f) *Monitor and evaluate results;* (g) *Celebrate if successful; if not, return to step 3 and repeat the process.* Each one of these steps is vital to a cogent equity audit being initiated and implemented within the school. Here, we believe steps 2–6 are undergirded by the technocratic skills of the school administrators, and steps 1 and 7 are stages that require school leaders to have a predisposition to involving the communities of their respective schools—more humanistic than technocratic. Therefore, when conducting equity audits, it is crucial for school leaders to involve relevant stakeholders in the process (i.e., steps 1 and 7). This entails school administrators to not be close-minded when it comes to acknowledging the community as playing a vital part in the educative process of their students.

Become Proactive in Engaging the Community

As we have stated throughout this chapter as well as the book, if school leaders want to improve their schools, it vitally important that they develop or cultivate their skillsets to enhance their community engagement. Thus, we would like to return to Skrla et al.'s (2009) equity audit steps, specifically step 1, which calls on school leaders to *create a committee of relevant stakeholders*, and step 7, which asks of school leaders to *celebrate if successful* the improvement of school policies and procedures as they relate to teacher, programmatic, and student achievement audits. We believe that these two steps are the underpinnings of becoming proactive in engaging the community. And when it comes to creating a committee of relevant stakeholders, Skrla et al. (2004) claimed the following:

> The first step [in conducting equity audits] is to put together a committee of relevant stakeholders, such as a group of teachers or a group of representatives of both educators and parents. What needs to be looked for here are individual stakeholders who will collaborate in carrying out the process. It is important to identify individuals who are respected by the groups they represent and who are also people of good will who would be open to dialogue and work focused on equity. (p. 151)

We would also suggest that in addition to educators and community members being open to dialogue, school leaders themselves should also recognize discourse as critically important when attempting to engage the community. Miller et al. (2011) have found that dialogue between school leaders and community members is a necessity for school improvement and should not be taken for granted by those in power. Freire (1970) maintained that "Dialogue cannot exist in the absence of a profound love for the world and for people . . . Love is at the same time for foundation of dialogue and dialogue itself" (p. 89). Miller et al. (2011) interpreted this form of "dialogical love" that Freire referred to as being undergirded by "humility, faith in the people, hope, critical thinking, and, ultimately, solidarity" (p. 1082). Miller et al. went on to indicate that Freire's notion of "dialogical love" entails "a deeper, richer engagement than is commonly inferred in haphazard calls for 'dialogue' in modern schooling context."

The conflation of Freire's (1970) "dialogical love" and Miller et al.'s (2011) critical interpretation of it leads us to expand Skrla et al.'s (2004) notion of dialogue with regard to equity audits. Yes, it is critically important that community members are open for dialogue; nevertheless, it is ultimately the school leader who is extending the invitation to community members to participate in equity audits that are undergirded by critical dialogue. Research has shown that one of the primary reasons many parents, especially those from urban communities, do not participate in parent meetings and other school-sponsored events is due to teacher intimidation. Many parents from these communities choose to remain on the sidelines because teachers often act with a territorial disposition toward parents whom they perceive to not have enough social and cultural capital. If indeed the school leader sets the tone of the school culture and climate, the onus is on the school leaders themselves to eradicate such hostile attitudes among educators. And we do not believe that it is an overstatement to stress that the notion of "dialogical love" is at stake.

Whether it is through solidarity or an insurgency model with the community, school leaders must galvanize faculty and staff to engage in tough talk that is undergirded by humility, respect, and love. Once again, in the spirit of openness, the community must also be made aware of the successes and failures of policies and procedures that impact student achievement, which intersects with step 7 of Skrla et al.'s (2009) equity audits. Many would argue that Freire's (1970) concept of "dialogical love" is rather simple to implement, but we would ask why it is not being practiced on a large scale.

Become Risk Takers and Innovators in Meeting the Needs of the Students and Community

Ordinarily, when the terms "risk taking" and "innovation" are mentioned in relation to building bridges with the community, one normally expects the operationalization of tangible and palpable skillsets to accompany the notion of taking risks and being innovative. Such skillsets might include the ability to galvanize support from faculty, staff, and the community to extend school hours to increase student achievement as well as ensure that students are free from many of the peer pressures that accompany certain communities. Ron Ferguson (2008) from Harvard University has found in his extensive research that the extended school day is a viable option to increase academic achievement. And we certainly suggest that school leaders take such research into consideration when trying to increase academic achievement and better connect with the community.

Other skillsets regarding risk taking and innovation might also include the abilities to increase parental involvement through pioneering measures and restructure the curricula to ensure a holistic approach to the educative process. We readily recognize that such tangible skillsets are a prerequisite to increasing community involvement and ensuring that all students are successful. But when it comes to risk taking and innovation, we would like to add a more intangible skillset to the toolbox of education leaders. Thus, we would like to once again return to Freire's (1970) research as well as the research by Miller et al. (2011) on community engagement. We believe that when it comes to school leaders engaging in risk taking and innovation with the community, the tangible skillsets needed to move the school forward will become more transparent when school leaders develop a sense of *faith* in their communities. This is ultimate risk taking and innovation on the part of the school leader.

When social and cultural capital is in abundant supply among stakeholders, it is somewhat easy for school leaders to have a sense of faith in their communities. The problem with faith in the community arises when the stakeholders as a whole are perceived to lack such cultural and social capital, as with the issue of parental involvement. Earlier, we mentioned that when it comes to school leaders being proactive in engaging the community, it is critically important for them to be open to dialogue. In order for the "dialogical love" that Freire spoke of to exist between the school leader and his or her community, the school administrator has to have "faith in the people" he or she has been charged to lead and work with on a daily basis (Freire, 1970; Miller et al., 2011).

We assert here that the notion of school leaders having *faith in the people* is not a stretch when it comes to school leaders being risk takers and innovators. We do not mean to suggest that school leaders having faith in the community is a risk-taking adventure with regard to such stakeholders not being trustworthy. What we are suggesting is that school leaders need a liberatory consciousness awakening while abandoning their sense of certitude to find such faith. School leaders abandoning their certitude is in essence the risk taking and innovation that occurs as they build bridges with their communities. "The absence of this faith promotes leadership that is rooted in notions of domestication and 'assistencialism'—a condition of dependence that is often created and sustained when systems and institutions do not engage emergent community capacities" (Miller et al., p. 1083). Miller et al. went on to opine that "with such humility and faith, dialogue centers the contextual expertise of the people as active advocates for social transformation" (p. 1083). Thus, the humility and faith that Freire (1970) emphasized that educators and school leaders must have toward the community in essence produces transformation in the community that is undergirded by the school leader's own sense of risk taking and innovation. School leadership programs have to find a way to support the marriage of humanistic risk taking and innovation (i.e., faith in the people) with the technical side of such endeavors we alluded to earlier. Such a conflation is what is needed to tackle the myriad issues and problems confronting schools across the nation.

Conclusion

Building bridges with the community is a prerequisite for school success. Throughout this chapter, we have identified several ways in which school leaders can become better bridge builders with their respective communities. We started the chapter by indicating that if school leaders are to become bridge builders, there is a certain amount of reflection that has to take place among them. The ethics of critique, care, and justice were utilized as a framework for school leaders to consider in their endeavors to serve the community. We also made the recommendation to school leaders to establish community networks to ascertain community perceptions and perspectives. Here, we illuminated the need for school leaders to form partnerships with faith-based institutions. These organizations have been at the vanguard of fighting for social justice and equality. The insurgency model was suggested as a way for school leaders to connect with such religious institutions and benefit from their stalwart support for justice. Nevertheless, a caveat was offered to school leaders when forming such an insurgency with religious institutions: to retain their voice in the dialogue and not acquiesce to edicts of the church that might go against the school's proclamations of ensuring that all students are respected and able to achieve academically.

In building bridges with the community, we also suggested that school leaders become proficient in conducting action research and equity audits. We pulled from Skrla et al. (2004, 2009) equity audit models to illuminate how beneficial equity audits can be in uncovering inequities within school policies and procedures. Humanistic as well as technical skills are both critical in bridge building. And we certainly believe that equity audits and action research increase those technical skills that school administrators desperately need in order to improve education for all students.

The utilization of equity audits was also suggested as way for school leaders to become proactive with the community. We found Skrla et al.'s (2004, 2009) steps to successful equity audits appealing as far as being proactive in engaging the community. Step 1, in particular, calls on school leaders to *create a committee of relevant stakeholders* when conducting equity audits. It would be a critical mistake and even educational malpractice for school leaders not to consider individuals from the community as having a voice in equity audits. Such participation from community members helps to cultivate trust between them and school leaders.

And finally, we advocated risk taking and innovation on the part of school leaders to meet the needs of students and their communities; we believe that this is vitally important for school leaders in successfully engaging their communities. When it comes to risk taking and innovation, we advocate school leaders exhibit faith in the people, which is a necessity, especially faith in those who do not have what school administrators consider an abundant supply of social and cultural capital. We suggest that such faith in the people will manifest in tangible and concrete innovations that will ultimately lead to better relationships between school leaders and the individuals they have been charged to care for.

5

Language, Liberty, and Leading for Diversity at Payton High

(Case Study)

Introduction

Payton High School (PHS) is a somewhat diverse school, which has been witness to enormous change over time. It was once a predominantly White school until the American Civil Rights Movement and subsequent laws changed the school's homogeneous racial makeup. Federal law and public outcry from African Americans forced the school to start enrolling African Americans and other students of color. For example, a Consent Decree from the state ordered that PHS address the overrepresentation of students of color in special education and make an earnest effort to hire more teachers and administrators of color (see McCray et al., 2008). PHS had a tradition of administrators and many teachers who spent their entire careers at the school. Payton High School is one of the larger schools in Westland County. It serves approximately 800 students in grades 9–12. The demographic makeup of the school is about 50% White, 30% African

School Leadership in a Diverse Society, pages 77–85
Copyright © 2014 by Information Age Publishing
All rights of reproduction in any form reserved.

American, 15% Hispanic, and the rest of the students are classified as Other (Asian, American Indian, multiracial, etc.). The teaching staff includes 44 teachers and 3 administrators (1 principal and 2 assistant principals). The school had a long history of serving the interests of the White majority. The freedom struggles of the Civil Rights Movement brought changes to the well-entrenched Jim Crow laws that reinforced the legalized segregation of that time period. This part of the South was no stranger to segregation, but the change in this part of the state was less revolution and more evolution. PHS, like many others in the South, dragged its feet with regard to fully accepting students of color, but over time it did. Eventually, the school began to also hire teachers of color. Although many things have changed, many of the biases of past generations are now hidden by smiles and cordiality. The bigotry and hate that was once overt is now covert, but all that is needed is an incident to spark its return.

Principal Fred Jones

The expectation for a long career and retirement from PHS was no different for Fred Jones, who was born in the local community and graduated from Payton High. He had the opportunity to move away from the Payton community to attend college, teach for a time while earning his master's in educational leadership, and eventually returned to PHS to become the principal, which was a lifelong dream. For Fred, this was a dream come true. However, Fred's tenure as principal has not been without a few unique challenges. A few years back, there was a major conflict at the school and in the community when the issue of same-sex dating at the prom came up. Two years later, when Payton's legendary assistant principal, Gene Johnson retired, Fred saw an opportunity for Payton to hire its first administrator of color. What Fred did not expect was two candidates of color and a split decision from the committee that was charged to advise Fred. Due to some politics at the central office and in the local community, Chris Thomas became the school's first African American assistant principal. Fred's superintendent, Kenneth Wilson, was quite pleased with the decision, even remarking, "With the hiring of Chris, Payton High School has proven to be leading the way in diversity." Fred was a bit less enthusiastic, as he felt that the other candidate was more of the instructional leader that PHS really needed. Nevertheless, Fred welcomed Mr. Thomas to the administrative team as an assistant principal. Completing the administrative team was assistant principal Richard "Dick" Beard, known to friends as "Old D.B." He was a 25-year veteran educator known more for his talk than his actions, but he was generally a nice guy and well-liked in the community.

The Liberty Act

The Payton community also was in flux. A large number of Hispanic families were beginning to settle in the area; some were transient families who came to work in the local fields, but others were middle-class families who made the local community their home while commuting to work in nearby Central City. The political climate of the day also complicated matters. During this time period, the entire country was debating the issue of illegal immigration, with strong feelings on both sides. Many national politicians and locally based community organizers helped to create the Liberty Act, which was aimed at better facilitating the process for immigrants to become U.S. citizens. It would grant "transitional" residency status to deportable alien students who came to the United States as children and had since graduated from high school. This bill would grant full citizenship if the student went on to graduate from an accredited institution of higher learning or was to complete honorably an enlistment contract with a branch of the military. The Liberty Act also caused high emotion in the local community, as its opponents and proponents squared off in town hall meetings, debates down the road at the University of Mannesville, and on the Internet. Even still, there was a general feeling in the community that it was a safe haven, largely insulated from the "craziness" of outsiders. Little did the Payton community know, but these larger debates and clashes would find their way into the high school.

The Incident

The incident took place in the classroom of seasoned eleventh-grade English teacher, Ms. Harper. On this particular day, she was showing a DVD of *Romeo and Juliet* and sitting at her desk grading papers. Most of the students were paying attention, with a couple using the opportunity to catch up on some other assignment. There were also a few who used the time to get some sleep. Ms. Harper had the reputation as a teacher who favored students who participated, and ignored those who didn't. As the movie continued, students wrote down notes. At some point, Juan, who came to PHS as a freshmen, got up to throw away some paper. As he returned to his seat, he was told, "You are blocking my view. I can't see the film" by fellow classmate Mary Louise, who was sitting behind him. Juan, whose parents worked as executives just outside of Central City in the new Jupiter auto plant, replied, "I'm about to sit down, thank you." Mary Louise then in a low tone stated, "Think you run the country." A verbal exchange then ensued, with Juan saying, "¡Déjame en paz! (Leave me alone!) in an exasperated tone of voice. At this point, Mary Louise demanded an apology from Juan. She insisted that he called her a derogatory name, and Mary Louise began to cry. Ms. Harper finally took notice of what was going on as the film continued to play. She demanded that Juan leave the classroom, exclaiming, "Juan, leave Mary Louise alone and go to Mr. Thomas' office now! Do not come back to this classroom until you can control yourself!" Juan, usually quiet and attentive in class, had been brought up to respect teachers and other school officials. He attempted to tell his version of the story to Ms. Harper, but she left him no choice but to reluctantly comply and head directly to the office of Mr. Thomas, all the while feeling as if he was being wronged.

Administrative Reaction

Juan waited patiently outside of Mr. Thomas' office. Little did Juan know that Dick Beard had already gotten Mary Louise's version of the story as she left the room shortly after she burst into tears, clearly distraught from the incident. Old D.B. was now reporting the "facts" to Mr. Thomas. "Look Chris, I'm not telling you how to discipline these kids, but in my years of experience, I learned that you gotta nip this kind of thing in the bud! We can't have these kids causing all kinds of classroom disruptions." He continued, "You should see that poor girl crying her eyes out. And I don't need to remind you that this is one of your first big discipline situations, Chris, and the central office 'hot shots' are all wondering how you are gonna handle things as they come up."

Mr. Thomas replied, "Thanks Dick for giving me the inside scoop. I think I know what I have to do."

Dick smiled and before he left, stated, "All right Chris, you are the man! We are glad you are here; I think the board made a really good decision when they hired you. If I don't see you later on today, I will see you at the game tonight." Dick left and Juan soon entered. Chris knew that Juan had transferred to Payton High School from an international school in Mexico City, but wasn't sure if Juan had been enrolled in the school's recently expanded English as a Second Language (ESL) program. In fact, Juan was bilingual, speaking English and Spanish fluently. Chris had noticed that when he first came to the school, Juan had had a little difficulty finding his niche socially. His good grades earned him a place in the after-school Debate Club, but he seemed most comfortable hanging out with a wide mix of other Spanish-speaking students in the halls and cafeteria. Although he was surprised by Juan's uncharacteristic behavior, Chris felt the need to handle the incident decisively.

Chris, with a stern look on his face, said, "I'm surprised to see you in my office . . . would you like to tell me what you are doing here?" Juan, who was already disenchanted, sat quietly and shrugged his shoulders. Mr. Thomas went on to say, "Anyway, I know why you are here, but tell me what happened." Juan began to recount the story, but Mr. Thomas interrupted at a certain point, "Look, why didn't you just sit down and let it go?"

Juan, with a puzzled look said, "Mr. Thomas, I am here to get a good education, and I don't have to put up with this racist crap. Why does she think we feel that we run this country? That girl is stupid, and I don't see why you are sitting there taking her side, especially since you are Black. What if she would have said, 'You Blacks think you run the country,' what would you have done?"

Chris, who misread Juan's statement, was immediately offended by his overt mention of race. His anger and preconceived notions blocked him from listening to the entire context. He retorted, "What did you say? You Blacks? How about you think about this incident at home for a few days?" Without stopping to hear further details from Juan or to interview Mary Louise, Mr. Thomas gave Juan a two-day suspension for the verbal altercation with Mary Louise and what he felt was insubordination. At this point, Juan was totally disheartened and felt abandoned by the school. When he got home, he immediately told his parents and family members about what happened in the classroom and with Mr. Thomas. Moments after Juan left his office, Mr. Thomas realized that he had neglected to inform Juan's parents of the two-day suspension. He wasn't sure if they spoke English, and he certainly didn't speak Spanish, but, with a sigh, he reached for the phone. Just then the school secretary came to let him know his next appointment had arrived. He placed the phone back on the hook. As he went to greet his next visitors, it occurred to him that he'd heard something recently about Mary Louise and the Debate Club. Hadn't she abruptly decided to quit midsemester?

Community Reaction

Juan's parents worked outside of the local community but were interested and active in local politics and events. Juan's aunt Maria was heavily involved in organized support for the Liberty Act and Latino issues. When she caught wind of what happened from Juan's parents, she immediately made the connection to the larger opposition to the recent influx of Latinos into the community, attacks on bilingual education, and immigration reform. Juan's parents were puzzled and more than a little upset that Mr. Thomas had not informed them directly of the incident, and they decided to voice their concerns at the next school board meeting. Maria even threatened to call the local newspaper and "inform them about the insidious disciplinary policies and procedures at Payton High," as she described it.

Mary Louise also told her parents about what occurred, claiming that Juan had sworn at her in an angry tone. It just so happened that her parents were staunch opponents of the Liberty Act and firmly believed that schools should teach English only. They opposed the burgeoning ESL program at the school, feeling that the funds would be better spent on programs for students who already knew how to speak English. They interpreted this incident as yet another in a long line of encroachments on the integrity and traditional values of the local community. They felt the suspension was not only justified, but an apology should also come along with it. Mary Louise's dad, Chuck, exclaimed, "That darn school ain't what it used to be when I went there. I should go up there and give them a good piece of my mind."

The Next Day

The next day, teachers could tell that something was going on as the student grapevine began spreading rumors. There was a rumor that an angry assembly of Hispanics planned to converge on tomorrow's school board meeting. There was another rumor that a group vehemently opposed to the Liberty Act planned a march that would end at the high school with a big rally. There was even talk of executives and workers at the Jupiter plant not being happy about the recent events at Payton High and the Vice President of Diversity paying a visit to superintendent Kenneth Wilson. Unfortunately, as the rumors spread, the real story faded further into the background. By midmorning, Dick Beard visited the office of Chris Thomas. Dick exclaimed, "What in the heck happened yesterday? I come to work and there's talk of protests and rallies!"

Chris responded, "Hey Dick, don't look at me, I just did my job, it's as simple as that."

"Yeah, but what are you going to tell Fred?" Chris paused at this point. Then a teacher, Sonya Hernandez, walked into the room. She was a biracial (African American and Mexican American) Spanish-speaking teacher who was in her second year of teaching ESL. She excused herself for interrupting, but she needed to speak to Mr. Thomas. Dick quickly said, "Please come in Ms. Hernandez, I was just leaving." Dick looked back at Chris and said, "Think about what you will say to you-know-who."

Ms. Hernandez got right to the point, stating, "Mr. Thomas, I know you are rather new to this position and this school, so am I. I feel like there is a lot of tension in the air around here and in the local community. I wanted you to know that I know Juan and his family very well, and I can't help but think that there is some more to the story here. I am not questioning your administrative decision, but rather I am asking that we all slow things down and figure out what is a school-related incident versus broader agendas that feed off of such an incident." Mr. Thomas then began to reflect on everything that happened up until that point. He wondered about whether or not he gave Juan a fair opportunity to tell his story, he questioned the advice and wisdom of old Dick Beard, and he really wondered about what principal Fred Jones would say. Before he could say anything, he looked up and Fred was in his doorway. Fred greeted Ms. Hernandez and asked Mr. Thomas if he could have a word with him once they were done.

Fred's Dilemma

Fred got a chance to talk to Chris about the situation. By this time, Fred too was also hearing rumors. He felt like he had been blindsided by all that was going on. He had experienced this feeling before with the same-sex dating issue at the prom and the controversial hiring decision involving Mr. Thomas. Fred was familiar with making tough decisions and dealing with different stakeholders, but each situation was different. Deep in his heart, Fred did really care about the school and the local community. He was a product of its lessons and nurturing. At the same time, he knew that time brings change, and all educators are charged with creating safe, effective, and equitable educational environments for all students. Which side wins when traditional community values collide with the reality of 21st century diversity (new people, language, cultures, etc.)? How should Fred deal with Mr. Thomas, who was not his first choice as the person to fill the position of assisstant principal (and now he sees why)? What can Fred do to avoid or address the rumored rallies and protests?

Discussion Notes

This case is one that combines a number of complex educational and community issues. It deals with student discipline, diverse learners, school-community relations, and leadership for educational equity. School discipline continues to be a major issue in U.S. K–12 education. How can effective learning take place if there is disruption, chaos, and/or disarray? Thus, classroom management and disciplinary policies are put into place to enhance the learning environment. Unfortunately, while educational policies themselves may not seem biased, their impact can result in the targeting of students of color. For instance, many in K–12 education are aware of the disproportionate number of African American male students placed into special education. In addition, students of color are disciplined more often and more harshly than their White peers, many times for subjective reasons. Therefore, it is reasonable to conclude that seemingly neutral educational policies have serious implications for certain racial/ethnic groups. Even more important is the idea that the policies and their implementation contribute to an environment that allows certain behaviors. In this case, there was a certain kind of school culture that allowed the situation to occur and then escalate so quickly. The responsibility for creating educational environments that promote excellence and equity falls squarely on the shoulders of educational leaders.

This case also deals with school-community issues. Education does not occur in isolation. Many times, schools are intimately connected to the communities in which they reside. In this case, we find the community in a state of flux. On the one hand, it seeks to maintain its traditions, history, and past practices, but on the other hand must deal with demographic, economic, and political change. The broader debates over the Liberty Act reflect the attitudes that abound in the local community. The incident in the school is connected to these overarching debates. Once again, it is up to teachers and educational leaders to deal with these issues at the school level and sometimes create forums for teaching and learning for the broader community.

The multiple issues presented in this case are overlapping and happen quickly in the daily life of a school. Thus, educational leaders are constantly "putting out fires," working with different groups, and responding to an ever-changing dynamic educational environment. Sometimes reflection is sacrificed for reaction, as we saw in this case. This is why educational leaders should be reflective practitioners who place educational excellence and equity at the forefront of their decision making. Emphasis on excellence keeps high standards, accountability, vision, and focus paramount in the minds of leaders. The equity dimension encourages fair treatment of all groups, rejection of stereotypes, and the promotion of safe and effective learning environments for all. In this case, just like in K–12 education today, leadership is critical.

Questions

Discipline

1. Chris Thomas was chosen as assistant principal because the hiring committee believed that he would be an effective disciplinarian, particularly with African American students. What did he do well

in handling this discipline incident with Juan? What could he have done differently?

2. If you were Fred Jones, how would you counsel Mr. Thomas on his handling of the current incident? Future incidents? Would you counsel Dick Beard? If so, how?

3. This incident originated in the classroom of Ms. Harper. How could she have better organized her classroom procedures to lessen the chance of such an incident? How could she have handled the situation differently?

Diversity

1. As the student demographics of Payton High School continue to evolve, what do you think Fred Jones should do for his current faculty and staff to enhance their skills and abilities to serve students better? Given the multiple and competing demands on teacher preparation time and in-service days, what professional development (if any) should be planned or provided?

2. As the opportunity presents itself due to attrition and retirement, should Fred Jones make any adjustments in procedures for hiring new faculty and staff? If so, how?

3. Describe how examples of bias or discrimination happened at the individual, institutional, and societal levels?

Community Relations

1. How should Fred Jones communicate with Juan's parents? Once the news of the incident reaches the wider community, should Fred communicate with the whole school community? If so, how?

2. Fred knows that there is a wider debate going on in the community regarding the Liberty Act, Latinos, and access to opportunities. What role, if any, should Payton High School have in this debate? How can Fred turn this incident into a teachable moment?

3. How can Fred and his administration diffuse the high tensions running in the community and get to the truth of what actually happened?

Note: Third authorship credit goes to Anne Marie FitzGerald, who worked diligently on this chapter. Anne Marie is a doctoral student in the Educational Leadership program at Lehigh University, Bethlehem, Pennsylvania.

SECTION **III**

6

Using Culturally Relevant Leadership to Address Cultural Collision and Collusion in Urban Schools

Educational inequality offers one measure to gauge the persistent and pervasive problem of racial inequality. The persistent problem of segregation in schools, the inequitable funding of schools in poor neighborhoods, gaps in academic achievement, and the further entrenchment of a Eurocentric curriculum are examples of racial inequality in education. We assert that applying a race-conscious theory to understanding these problems will move us further along the path towards securing greater racial equality.

—Zamudio, Russell, Rios, & Bridgeman, 2011, p. 2

Leaders are shaped in part by the context in which they lead. By context I mean the different environments and settings wherein leaders engage with others. Successful leaders are often able to effect changes in context, which are prerequisites for altering what is and creating the conditions for what could be. Whether results are positive or negative depends on many factors... Understanding context is essential to principals' and superinten-

School Leadership in a Diverse Society, pages 89–108

dents' ability to develop strategies for leading change and improvement in urban schools and school districts.

—Payzant, 2011, p. 1

Together, both of these quotes provide acute insight into today's educational plight and subsequent leadership challenge. The problems are indeed persistent in that they remain almost like permanent fixtures in schools. Achievement gaps, low graduation rates, high truancy, low standardized test scores, race-based tracking policies, irrelevant curriculum, student (and teacher) apathy, and overrepresentation of students of color in special education continue to plague schools (especially urban schools) (Beachum & McCray, 2011; Epps, 2005; Kunjufu, 2002; Lynch, 2006; McKinsey & Company, 2009; Obiakor, 2008; Obiakor & Ford, 2002; Perry, 2003; Skiba & Peterson, 1999). These complicated issues require educational leaders who can deal effectively with politics, policy, perceptions, and people. At the same time, these leaders must have a coherent vision and continuously improve the school's climate for the purpose of increased student learning. This is by no means an easy task. In order to both deal with pervasive and persistent problems and align leadership to context, a framework is needed to facilitate desired outcomes. The purpose of this chapter is to propose culturally relevant leadership as a framework for educational leaders for personal change and organizational improvement. In addition, we seek to apply culturally relevant leadership toward persistent and pervasive educational problems as entailed in the concepts of cultural collision and collusion (Beachum & McCray, 2004, 2008a).

Today's School Leadership

Today's educational leaders must be visionary, organized, fiscally responsible, reflective, engaged, and politically savvy (Beachum & Obiakor, 2005; Scheurich & Skrla, 2003). Budget constraints in many school districts across the nation are forcing educational leaders to make some tough decisions about layoffs, closing buildings, and reduction of resources. At the same time, they are dealing with increasing pressures for accountability and high standardized test scores while trying to keep stable student enrollments and maintain a culture of excellence. The context has changed, forcing educators to behave differently by rethinking current practice and carefully examining the needs of students in the 21st century.

As educational leaders deal with numerous local issues, they must also keep in mind the connection to the wider world. The world of today is marked by unprecedented access to knowledge and technological innovation. Innovation and technology has the capacity to change our lives in exciting ways, but we need the kind of schools that encourage innovation and experimentation. Similarly, access to knowledge and technological advancement has given us the ability to communicate and collaborate in new and incredible ways, never imagined by previous generations. Even new terminology has been created, with terms like "global village" and "internationalism" (Friedman, 2005; Scholte, 2000). Thus, our students must not only be prepared to work well with others domestically, but also globally. At the same time, this creates new problems with regard to overseas outsourcing of jobs, global competition, and not to mention increasing automation (Pink, 2006). Educational speaker and consultant Tony Wagner (2008) said the following:

> In today's highly competitive global "knowledge economy," all students need new skills for college, careers, and citizenship. The failure to give all students these new skills leaves today's youth—and our country—at an alarming competitive disadvantage. Schools haven't changed; the world has. And our schools are not failing. Rather, they are obsolete—even the ones that score the best on standardized tests. This is a very different problem requiring an altogether different solution. (p. xxi)

The framing of educational problems and search for solutions are largely within the realm of educational leaders. These leaders are the ones who impact the culture of the educational organization, thereby influencing the people in the organization. They are also the ones who must provide an environment in which students can exercise their minds in order to be creative and excel academically. In addition, they must provide a local and global vision that deals with immediate issues yet looks to the future. Although this local/global perspective is vitally important, so is recognizing the steady trend of increasing social and cultural diversity impacting K–12 schools.

Demographic Changes in K–12 Education

As we have mentioned previously, the demographic forecast for the United States is one of increasing diversity. This can influence curricular content, teaching approaches, resource allocation, and leadership strategies.

> While children of color constituted about one-third of the student population in 1995, they are expected to become the numerical majority by 2035. This change will render the expression "minority students" statistically inaccurate. By 2050, so-called minorities will collectively account for nearly 57 percent of the population. (Hodgkinson, 1998, p. 3)

In places such as California, Hawaii, Mississippi, New Mexico, Texas, and the District of Columbia, students of color have become the majority with regard to K–12 student enrollments (NCES, 1998). Part of the issue here is that while the student population is becoming more diverse, the current cadre of teachers (Mizialko, 2005) and administrators (Tillman, 2003) in schools are overwhelmingly White.

This homogeneity in many American K–12 schools is juxtaposed with the demographic changes occurring in the United States. The result in many cases could be more cultural insensitivity, lackluster teaching, and apathetic leadership. The all-too-common "I see children, not color" rhetoric is sure to be challenged by calls for power-sharing over politics, substance over style, and real progress over pandering. White females make up 72.5% of all preschool and kindergarten teachers (Calculator, 2010). Recognizing how this unfolds in urban education, Hancock (2006) wrote,

> The reality that White women are on the front lines of urban education is clearly evident. While we continue to recruit and retain minority teachers, it is critical that we also focus our attention on helping to educate White women teachers about the realities of teaching students who may hold a different sociopolitical, sociocultural, and socioeconomic perspective. (p. 97)

This is not to overstate the point that we must have teachers of color teaching students of color or say that White teachers should only teach White students. More important is the attitude and expectations of teachers and school leaders. Teachers of color are not always successful with students of color; these teachers too, can have low expectations (Kunjufu, 2002). This is why things like worldview, attitude, perspective, and ideology are so important in education. Many K–12 educators and theorists have long supported the notion that educators should be neutral (Cunningham & Cordeiro, 2003). This applies to everything from their political views to teaching approaches and opinions. We assert that this adherence to educational or pedagogical neutrality is unproductive, if not impossible. Our actions in educational institutions serve some purpose or follow an agenda, whether we like it or not. Starratt (1991) reminds us that all social arrangements have some purpose, and schools are no different. In fact, they usually serve the interests of those in power and underserve the interests of those with less power (Zamudio et al., 2011). Villegas and Lucas (2002b) discussed the notion of sociocultural consciousness and dyconsciousness. Sociocultural consciousness encompasses an understanding that differences in social location are not neutral. In all social systems, some positions are accorded greater status than others. With this status differentiation comes differential access to power. Because differences in access to power profoundly influence one's experience in the world, prospective teachers [and school leaders] need to comprehend how American society is stratified, for example, along racial/ethnic, social class, and gender lines... They need to critically examine the role that schools play in this reproduction and legitimation process. (p. 22)

This kind of awareness recognizes students' histories and communities, respects the knowledge they bring to class, and uses this knowledge to hone and improve the teaching process. Conversely, sociocultural dyconsciousness supports a deficit perspective. With this view, Villegas and Lucas (2002b) explained that

Teachers [and school leaders] looking through the deficit lens believe that the dominant culture is inherently superior to the cultures of marginalized groups in society. Within this framework, such perceived superiority makes the cultural norms of the dominant group the legitimate standard for the United States and its institutions. Cultures that are different from the dominant norm are believed to be inferior... Such perceptions inevitably lead teachers to emphasize what students who are poor and of color cannot do rather than what they already do well. (p. 37)

This further supports the point that what we believe impacts what we do, whether that is teaching in the classroom or leading entire school buildings. Many have long supported the notion that teacher expectations have an influence on student learning and achievement (Irvine, 1990; Obiakor et al., 2012; Rist, 1970; Rosenthal & Jacobson, 1969). The problem is that far too many teachers and educational leaders have had low expectations for so long that cultures of failure and apathy pervade many schools. In educational leadership in particular, leader attitude and perspective is a vital key to success.

Educational Leadership: Past and Present

In educational leadership, the sociocultural dyconsciousness is sometimes cloaked in other terminology. Educational leadership is frequently infused with business ideas, management theories, and organizational development approaches. All of these can contribute to better and more effective schools. But as these notions are embraced, they cannot discount the fact that schools are first and foremost places where young people learn. Second, these ideas should not be used as a way to ignore the difficult issues of race/ethnicity, gender, class, and such. Educational leadership rests on the philosophical pillars of positivism, scientific management, and structuralism (English, 2008). Dantley (2005) agrees: "The scientific management paradigm that emphasizes quantifiable measures of success, rationality, predictability, and routinization has historically grounded educational leadership practice" (p. 652). The issue at hand is that these notions by themselves are not substantive enough for today's educational leaders. Dantley (2002) also asserted that educational leadership "has borrowed idioms and syntax from economics and the business world all in an effort to legitimate itself as a valid field" (p. 336). This is most likely due to the history and trajectory that supports and guides traditional educational leadership/administration.

As noted earlier, educational leadership/administration was developed on a foundation of business ideas and models and technical efficiency. Furthermore, the early days of the 20th century were times of widespread and extreme racism, sexism, homophobia, and xenophobia (Callahan, 1962; Karpinski & Lugg, 2006). One of the "founding fathers" of educational leadership was Elwood P. Cubberley. His writings were used to prepare many educational leaders. More pointedly, Karpinski and Lugg noted, "Between 1911 and 1945, Cubberley's educational history and administration texts were used to prepare generations of teachers and administrators" (p. 280). Unfortunately, his perspective embraced notions like Social Darwinism and did not embrace America's growing racial/ethnic diversity; in fact, in many cases, he saw it as a threat (Karpinski & Lugg, 2006). Under this umbrella of leadership preparation, standardization, "one size fits all" (Tyack, 1974), and Americanization were prominent ideas. At the same time, these ideas fit well within an overarching framework of male Anglo American racial superiority. Tyack and Hansot (1982) stated that Cubberley supported a belief in "the inherent superiority of white, male Anglo-Saxon, native-born Americans" (p. 127). Moreover, Cubberley enthusiastically upheld the American businessman (not woman) as the ethical, economic, political, and genetic role model that school leaders should emulate (Callahan, 1962). Similarly, educational leadership was influenced by other fields like educational psychology.

Educational leadership was heavily impacted by notions in educational psychology that encouraged the supremacy of quantitative measures and hierarchical control. Educational psychologist Edward Thorndike championed the idea that if something existed, then it could be measured (Cremlin, 1961). This bias toward empirical measurement had great attraction for the field of educational leadership/administration. Thus, early in the history of educational leadership, most were being trained to be well-versed in efficiency, to utilize business models in schools, and assess and evaluate according to quantitative methods (Karpinski & Lugg, 2006). Not surprisingly, these tendencies would explain why intelligence testing (and later standardized tests) became so important to these leaders and how this impacted their view of diversity.

The Legacy of Testing: Ghosts of the Past or Signposts for the Future

The field of educational leadership developed along with the use of standardized testing/intelligence tests. At this time, the United States was rife with notions of nationalism, eugenics, ethnocentrism/racism, sexism and misogyny, and ableism. In 1905, French psychologist Alfred Binet created the first intelligence test. "He believed that intelligence was too multidimensional to capture with a single number or score, and he worried that the use of his test would lead to inappropriate labeling of children" (Tatum, 2007, p. 42). Unfortunately, Binet's concerns were ignored when his test came to the United States (Gould, 1996). Henry Herbert Goddard was the first to translate Binet's test into English. He worked as the director of the Vineland Training School for Feeble-Minded Girls and Boys in New Jersey. Unlike Binet, Goddard "considered the test scores as measures of a single, innate entity, and his goal was to identify the mentally deficient, then segregate them and keep them from having children, in order to prevent the demise of American society" (Tatum, 2007, p. 44). It is worth noting that Binet's experimentation was in the early 20th century, and such a perspective was commonplace at this time. In addition, this was a time of a great influx of immigrants to the United States. Ironically, much of the "research" at this time reflected researcher bias more than it reflected sound methodology (Tatum, 2007). The bias was reflected in Goddard's own words when he wrote, "We cannot escape the general conclusion that these immigrants were of surprisingly low intelligence... We are now getting the poorest of each race" (as cited in Gould, 1996, p. 197). Lewis Terman would later apply Binet's test to American schools. This Stanford professor built upon Binet's work to create the Stanford-Binet Intelligence Scale. He was a supporter of eugenics, who wrote,

> No amount of school instruction will ever make them intelligent voters or capable citizens in the true sense of the word... The fact that one meets this type of frequency among Indians, Mexicans, and negroes suggest quite forcibly that the whole question of racial differences in mental traits will have to be taken up anew and by experimental methods... Children of this group should be segregated in special classes and be given instruction that is concrete and practical. They cannot master abstractions, but they can often

be made efficient workers, able to look out for themselves. There is no possibility at present of convincing society that they should be allowed to reproduce, although from a eugenic point of view they constitute a grave problem
because of their unusually prolific breeding. (Terman, 1916, pp. 91–92)

Today, these ideas seem not only outdated, but downright frightening.
We must also remember that these individuals were leading professors and
researchers at this particular time period. "Terman's test gave U.S. educators the first simple, quick, cheap, and seemingly objective way to 'track' students, or assign them to different course sequences according to perceived
ability" (Tatum, 2007, p. 47). This is the somewhat forgotten historical leg-
acy that undergirds intelligence and standardized testing. Furthermore, it
aligned with the dominant paradigm in educational leadership at that time.
Efficient administrators saw human differences in terms of deficiencies and
frequently labeled these differences as genetic and moral failings (Karpinski & Lugg, 2006, p. 281). This reflected the norm in school leadership at
this time and for many years to come.

In the aforementioned discussion, it is readily evident that there was
an overt bias against people based on their race/ethnicity. In the past, this
kind of bias was obvious. It reflected the general notion that people of color
were physically, mentally, emotionally, and biologically inferior to Whites. A
distinction between people of color and Whites was delineated. Psychologically, this created a binary in many people's minds that placed Whites (and
anything associated with Whites) on one end and Blacks (and anything associated with Blacks) on the other. This binary also operated as a spectrum
whereby anything close to White was affirmed and accepted and anything
close to Black was shunned and rejected (Perry, 2003). This critical information reveals the fact that things like textbooks, articles, and such from
Whites was (is) highly valued over the same things from people of color.
Thus, in educational leadership preparation, the professors, administrators, consultants, and others who train and educate future leaders have a
large influence on what they read and think. Unfortunately, messages of
bias and low expectations are continuously reinforced in more covert and
insidious ways in contemporary society. Perry (2003) noted,

Today, the ideology of Black intellectual inferiority is expressed in the media, which inserts itself into all aspects of our lives. The ideology of African
American inferiority is perhaps more robust today, in terms of its impact
on students, than it was in the pre–Civil Rights era...After all, we live in
the post–Civil Rights era. The society is now open. Few respectable people
will publicly assert that Black people are intellectually inferior. The visible,
in-your-face manifestations of oppression have been mostly eliminated. But

you can scarcely find a Black student who cannot recall or give you a litany of instances when he or she was automatically assumed to be intellectually incompetent. (p. 97)

Similarly, Tatum (1997) discussed the idea of cultural racism as "cultural images and messages that affirm the assumed superiority of Whites and the assumed inferiority of people of color" (p. 6). This line of thinking can lead to lowered expectations for students (and adults) of color. Therefore, today's educational leaders must do more than manage effectively, achieve high standardized test scores, and maintain the status quo. These things may help one keep their job, but they may not be helping all students in the school to maximize their potential and become successful. Another complicating factor in the educational leadership versus student success equation is context.

Urban School Context: Failure Versus Faith

Twenty-first century urban education appears to be confronted by a myriad of issues, problems, and complexities such as deindustrialization, lack of political influence, gang [wayward youth] violence, teen pregnancy, and drug abuse. Amid these overwhelming problems, many urban schools continue their undying mission of trying to educate all children who enter their doors. (Obiakor & Beachum, 2005, p. 3)

In recent years, there has been a rekindled interest in urban education as evidenced by the scrutiny placed on big-city superintendents, close examination of teaching practices, and greater interest in the successes and failures of students in these areas. This is further evidenced by books (Morris, 2009; Noguera, 2008; Obiakor & Beachum, 2005; Payzant, 2011); movies such as *Waiting for Superman* (2010); and television specials like *Heart of the City: Detroit's Dropout Factories* (2009). In the contemporary discussion regarding urban education, the word "urban" now had its own unique connotations. Not only is it used to describe a geographic locale in, near, or around major cities, but it also can be used as a term that signifies group categorization. Noguera (2008) expounded on the linguistic move toward urban when he wrote, "With the change of language that came about with the attempt to use more sensitive words to describe marginalized groups, urban is generally the more acceptable adjective used in reference to certain people who reside within certain neighborhoods in cities" (p. 23). This move was a purposeful departure from words like ghetto, barrio, and inner city. Furthermore, this change in language coincided with the broader changes in urban areas, especially in the United States.

The Devolution of Urban Areas

The decline of urban areas in the United States was less of a natural occurrence and more of a result of policies and practices. The downward spiral was evidenced as early as the latter 19th century as Midwestern and Northeastern cities witnessed a loss in industries such as clothing and furniture (Friedland, 1983). This early loss was followed by a series of decisions, policies, and developments that would create the urban areas of today and all that comes with this term. "Redlining" was a term that described the practice of literally drawing a red line on a map to designate areas where banks should not invest. These areas happened to be disproportionately Black neighborhoods and parts of cities. Wilson (2009) agreed, stating,

> Although many neighborhoods with a considerable number of European immigrants were redlined, virtually all black neighborhoods were excluded...This practice severely restricted opportunities for building or even maintaining quality housing in the inner city, which in many ways set the stage for the urban blight that many Americans associate with black neighborhoods. (p. 28)

Next, the strategic construction of freeways through many U.S. cities served to isolate African American communities. According to Wilson (2009), "Although these policies appeared to be nonracial, they facilitated the exodus of white working and middle-class families from urban neighborhoods and thereby indirectly contributed to the growth of segregated neighborhoods with high concentrations of poverty" (p. 30). Yet another example is Levittown-style tract housing, which made suburban living a reality (if not a possibility) for many working- and middle-class Americans (Noguera, 2008). The problem was that Levitt & Sons originally did not sell their homes to African Americans (Wilson, 2009). This facilitated the process of White transition to the suburbs while denying the same opportunity to Black people. Similarly, the suburban areas began to grow in population as well as political and economic power. They next took steps to "separate their financial resources and municipal budgets from cities" (Wilson, 2009, p. 31). Actions such as this not only further isolated urban residents, but would lay the groundwork for the funding and academic disparities we still see in urban schools, when compared with their suburban counterparts (Villegas & Lucas, 2002a). White flight describes a process by which "whites in many urban areas began to leave as the number of Blacks (and other people of color) increased" (Beachum & McCray, 2011, p. 14). As housing barriers and restrictions began to wane, middle-class Blacks began to move out of inner-city urban areas into majority White suburbs. Dyson (2004) called this process *Black trek*. The ramifications of this exodus were substantial. According to Wacquant (2001),

> Its economic basis has shifted from the direct servicing of the black community to the state, with employment in public bureaucracies accounting for most of the growth of professional, managerial and technical positions held by African Americans over the past thirty years. The genealogical ties of the black bourgeoisie to the black poor have also grown more remote and less dense. (p. 104)

This signaled the loss of community, as well as economic and political power. West (2008) warned,

> Once we lose any sense of a black upper or black middle class or a black upper working-class connecting with the black underclass with a "we" consciousness or sense of community, it becomes much more difficult to focus on the plight of the poor. (p. 57)

Not only would these events cause further isolation of urban areas, but it would also have "detrimental effects on communities and schools of color in the inner cities" (McCray & Beachum, 2011a, p. 14). The aforementioned occurrences provide keen sociohistorical insight and at the same time paints a vivid picture of how modern urban areas developed over time. Schools in these areas, of course, were not immune to these larger structural factors.

Contemporary Urban Schools: The Continuation of Structured Inequalities

The previous discussion illustrates the fact that policies and practices led to the development and maintenance of segregation between urban and suburban communities. In addition, this segregation is based on race/ethnicity and social class (i.e., Whites from people of color and wealthy from poorer communities). With regard to schools, "It is common knowledge that students who are poor and of color are overrepresented in urban schools and that suburban schools are attended largely by students who are white and more affluent" (Villegas & Lucas, 2002b, p. 45). In many cases, the differences between these schools are stark. First, there is the problem of outdated and dilapidated facilities. Kozol (2012) provided a vivid portrait of many urban schools with shattered windows, unsafe gyms, few computers, and insufficient or out-of-date textbooks. Next is the issue of qualified teachers. Villegas and Lucas (2002b) noted, "In addition to the unsafe and demoralizing facilities they offer their teachers, poorer inner-city districts generally pay teachers less than wealthy suburban school districts" (p. 47). This leads to the problem of finding teachers with proper content expertise. In addition, it leaves urban schools vulnerable, forcing them to hire people without proper certification and with less experience (Darling-Hammond, 1995). While policymakers and legislation like *No Child Left Behind* demand high quality teachers, many urban schools are lacking. For instance, in many high schools with large populations of students of color, up to 70% of math courses were taught by teachers who did not have math major or minor in college (Jerald, 2002). While logic would easily conclude that the students with the most need should get the most resources and best teachers, this is certainly not the case for many students in urban areas (Lewis, James, Hancock, & Hill-Jackson, 2008). Moreover, far too many teachers and educational leaders are plagued by deficit thinking. This perspective overtly or covertly supports a belief in the intellectual inferiority of students of color (Villegas & Lucas, 2002a). This notion further advocates that these deficiencies can be genetic or cultural. It also spawns a viewpoint that narrowly "blames the victim" and privileges the White, middle-class dominant culture. According to Larson and Ovando (2001), "When we use universal standards to judge student competence, without acknowledging disparities in either economic resources or opportunity, we consistently privilege the privileged" (p. 133).

In addition to the aforementioned issues, Wilson (2009) asserted that "Such [urban] schools have rigid district bureaucracies, poor morale among teachers and school principals, low expectations for students, and negative ideologies that justify poor performance" (p. 71). This does not obscure the role and responsibility that students have in the pursuit of their education. We assert that there are also larger structural factors that affect schooling beyond an individual's sphere of influence. As we examine schools more closely, we realize that there can be even more complex problems with regard to student-teacher interactions.

Cultural Collision and Collusion

The educational relationship and pact between the student and teacher is of extreme importance. Generally, teachers and school leaders who respect students' cultures, understand their communities, and are genuinely interested in students' lives are many times more successful than educators who may not (see Beachum & Dentith, 2004; Kunjufu, 2002; McCray & Beachum, 2011a; Milner, 2006; Theoharis, 2009; Villegas & Lucas, 2002b). We have developed two notions to describe problematic interactions between educators and students: cultural collision and cultural collusion. Cultural collision can be defined as the "clash in beliefs, cultures, or values" between youth and educators (Beachum & McCray, 2011, p. 2). Cultural collusion is when "educators implicitly usher out students who do not bring the proper social and cultural capital needed in school" (p. 69). In other words, when students of color may not be trying as hard or not working up to their potential, the teacher should do all that they can to encourage and inspire that student. In cultural collusion, the teacher (or even school leader) does the bare minimum or nothing at all at the cost of the student's educational opportunity. When this happens, they collude in an implicit educational agreement that dooms the student. It should be noted that these terms are related to the aforementioned broader urban context and educational discussion.

There are certain connections between our overarching discussion and the more specific discussion of these two concepts. First, the United States continues to become more diverse. If educators do not become more accepting of diversity, then there could be an increase in cases of cultural collision marked by continual instances of cultural insensitivity and miscommunication. Second, if school leaders do not embrace equity-based educational attitudes and approaches, then they may not be able to recognize or address when cultural collusion is at play. This also means that leadership preparation must continue to change and evolve from its origins or strict managerial and test-driven emphases to embrace new leadership perspectives (see Theoharis, 2009) and more comprehensive definitions of student success. When new leadership ideas are not utilized and/or forsaken for the status quo,

> it implicitly promotes transactional management by school leaders when it comes to the teaching and learning process instead of progressive transformational leadership—leadership designed to critique, interrogate, and unearth potential inequities within the school climate and culture that prohibits learning among all students. (McCray & Beachum, 2011a, p. 491)

Bryant and Jones (1993) asserted, "It is idealistic to think that contemporary school administrators can set things straight simply by directing teachers and students in a manner that may have worked a few decades ago" (p. 14). Third, the urban context itself creates an environment in which cultural collision and collusion could easily manifest. When educators are not invested in urban communities and make no attempt to better understand them, they create social and ideological barriers that facilitate cultural clash. Similarly, these same educators may harbor explicit or implicit deficit perspectives of urban students, thereby putting these students at risk of experiencing cultural collusion. Finally, the ever-present structural inequities inherent in our educational systems allow for cultural collision and collusion to occur. Students of color, especially in urban areas, are regularly undertaught, misplaced in special education, disproportionately suspended or expelled, and allowed to fail (Haberman, 2005; Kailin, 2002; Larson & Ovando, 2001; McCray & Beachum, 2006; Milner, 2010; Obiakor, Harris, & Beachum, 2009). As a way to lessen the impact of cultural collision and collusion and also address many of the other aforementioned issues, we offer a notion called Culturally Relevant Leadership.

Culturally Relevant Leadership for 21st Century Schools

Leadership in today's schools demands innovative thinking, contextual understanding, and the ability to engage diverse communities while negotiating complexity and ambiguity. This is not an easy endeavor. It also involves the realization that educators cannot keep on "doing things the way we have always done them." Thus, we suggest a framework known as Culturally Relevant Leadership. The authors have previously defined and discussed this notion in other publications (Beachum & McCray, 2012; McCray & Beachum, 2011a, 2011b). Broadly, in Culturally Relevant Leadership,

> the school leader starts with the "self" in freeing their minds and escaping the snares of the status quo. Leaders must then confront negative images and stereotypes resulting in a change in attitude. Finally, as reflective practitioners, they must change the way they operate on a daily basis. (McCray & Beachum, 2011a, p. 497)

Specifically, it rests on three tenets: liberatory consciousness, pluralistic insight, and reflexive practice. Philosophically, it is informed by Culturally Relevant Pedagogy, Advanced Change Theory, and Community Uplift Theory.

Philosophical Foundations for Culturally Relevant Leadership

Culturally Relevant Leadership is the result of preceding theories and philosophies. Some of these include Culturally Relevant Pedagogy, Advanced Change Theory, and Community Uplift Theory. First, is the concept that change begins with oneself, as evidenced in what is called Advanced Change Theory (ACT). This strategy aims at aligning the change agent with current reality while recognizing the organization/system as structural, political, technical, and moral (Beachum & Obiakor; 2005; Quinn & Snyder, 1999). In ACT, there is a belief in the leader or change agent that internal change will result in external change. Therefore, this effort starts with leadership making self-improvements and engaging in self-examination. This then allows the leader to model whatever they espouse, serving as an example in the organization. The intent is that when subordinates and others witness this process in the leadership, it will solicit them into a relationship in which they too can begin this process, thereby creating a community of change. As this process continues, the leader gains insight into the self, others, and the organization, eventually liberating oneself from the sanctions and limits in the system. This invites an inclination toward creative action, unconventional solutions, and provides broader strategic vision. The result is a change agent who is self-authorizing and independent-thinking, who is action-oriented, even in situations of complexity and ambiguity (Quinn & Snyder, 1999).

Second, we must acknowledge the idea that scholars have been consistent in their calls for educational approaches and classroom teaching that are culturally congruent with the learning styles of their student populations (Au & Kawakami, 1994; Lee, 1995; Milner, 2006; Shade, Kelly, & Oberg, 1997). Gloria Ladson-Billings (1994) established the notion of Culturally Relevant Pedagogy in her study of African American teachers who were deemed highly effective with their students. She described the concept as one that should be infused into the current curriculum for the purpose of "empowering students intellectually, socially, emotionally, and politically" (p. 18). She would later write about good teaching and would say that Culturally Relevant Pedagogy incorporated the following:

1. Students must experience academic success.
2. Students must develop and/or maintain cultural competence.
3. Students must develop a critical consciousness through which they challenge the status quo of the current social order (p. 160)

The final concept that undergirds Culturally Relevant Leadership is Community Uplift Theory (Beachum, Obiakor, & McCray, 2007). This notion advocates both individual and collective responsibility. With regard to the individual, it suggests that school leaders inspire self-determination and creativity in their students and teachers as well as in themselves. For instance, Kunjufu (2002) wrote, "You can observe Master Teachers after school, tutoring students and creating after-school clubs for chess, investment practice, computer skills, rap, rites of passage, newspaper reading, martial arts, and whatever other activities the students are interested in"

(p. 74). The collective aspect of Community Uplift Theory (CUT) promotes collaboration both "within schools and among schools" (Beachum et al., 2007, p. 275). This could include "high school students working with elementary schools, the computer teacher hosting a workshop for teachers who are new to using a computer, or groups of culturally diverse teachers from different grade levels [or schools] getting together to set goals or discuss problems" (Beachum et al., 2007, p. 275). An example of this in practice is an idea called educational rounds. This is when groups of educators (teachers, administrators, and concerned stakeholders) get together at an assigned time and place (like a Saturday morning) to discuss educational issues. The conversation is guided by an established protocol. The environment is purposely nonhierarchal and empowering. It privileges all involved, giving them a chance to express their opinions regardless of geographical location, position in the system, race/class/gender, or such. CUT also encourages the community to engage the school and not just the school reaching out to the community. These three philosophies establish the groundwork for the specific tenets of Culturally Relevant Leadership.

The Three Pillars of Culturally Relevant Leadership

Culturally Relevant Leadership rests on three tenets: liberatory consciousness, pluralistic insight, and reflexive practice. The first of these is liberatory consciousness, which "is akin to critical consciousness and seeks to raise awareness levels and increase knowledge with regard to diversity and social justice" (McCray & Beachum, 2011b, p. 92). Dantley and Tillman (2010) noted, "Leadership for social justice investigates and poses solutions for issues that generate and reproduce social inequalities" (p. 20). There is a long lineage of raising levels of consciousness from scholars and educators (Beachum & McCray, 2011a; Bogotch et al., 2008; Freire, 1970; Kailin, 2002; Marshall & Olivia, 2006; Ryan, 2006). This idea of consciousness raising is important because many may not be informed or concerned about inherent flaws and inequities embedded in our educational system (as noted in the discussion above). Villegas and Lucas (2002b) insightfully noted,

> Awareness of the pervasiveness and longevity of the inequities in schools and of the structures and practices that perpetuate them can be disheartening for prospective teachers [and school leaders]. But it is essential that they recognize these realities. If they see schools through the rose-colored glasses of the meritocratic myth, they will unwittingly perpetuate inequities. (p. 58)

Culturally relevant pedagogy supports liberatory consciousness here by promoting critical consciousness and cultural competence (Ladson-

Billings, 1995). The notion of liberatory consciousness is also informed by Advanced Change Theory and its emphasis on the change agent's effort to alter internal mindsets, transcend cognitive dissonance and stereotypes, and challenge personal hypocrisy (Quinn & Snyder, 1999). Advanced Change Theory also supports the leader confronting their own sources of personal resistance (e.g., the status quo, thinking that things can never really change, etc.) placing the common good ahead of self-gain. This focuses liberatory consciousness on the leadership and their quest toward personal liberation, so they might solicit others and serve as a role model.

> Completeness for the oppressed begins with liberation. Until liberation is achieved, individuals are fragmented in search of clarity, understanding, and emancipation. This liberation is not outside of us or created or accomplished through some external force. Rather, it begins with a change in thinking. (Milner, 2006, p. 85)

This change in thinking is when liberatory consciousness begins placing the leader on the course toward pluralistic insight, which highlights school leader's attitudes toward students. "It leans toward an affirming and positive notion of students (especially students of color) that acknowledges the uniqueness of their experiences and their rich diversity" (McCray & Beachum, 2011b, p. 92). The reality is that educators' (teachers and school leaders) expectations, attitudes, and dispositions are important components of the educational process (Beachum & McCray, 2008b; Irvine, 1990; Kunjufu, 2002; Lindsey, Roberts, & Campbell Jones, 2005; Obiakor, 2001). This is incredibly important because, as Tatum (2007) observed,

> Regardless of our own racial or ethnic backgrounds, we have all been exposed to racial stereotypes and flawed educational psychology, and unless we are consciously working to counter their influence on our behavior, it is likely that they will shape (subtly perhaps) our interactions with those who have been so stereotyped. (p. 52)

Thus, school leaders must actively examine their biases and attitudes to make sure that they are making decisions that will be for the best of all students. Beachum (2011) wrote, "Culturally relevant leaders should assist people in the organization to understand themselves and their students. This requires not only the appropriate knowledge base, but also the proper attitude especially when working with students of color and/or of different cultures/backgrounds" (p. 32). Pluralistic insight borrows directly from Culturally Relevant Pedagogy in that the former also advocates the alignment of leadership styles with the context and student population being led. Pluralistic insight also shares a common belief with Culturally Relevant Pedagogy that educators must truly believe in students of color in order for them to be successful.

The final tenet of Culturally Relevant Leadership is Reflexive Practice, which positions school leaders as "change agents who engage in ongoing praxis (reflection and action) for increased student success" (McCray & Beachum, 2011b, p. 92). This third concept also focuses on leadership actions, skills, and practice. In addition, "the work of the educator is not viewed as strictly objective, but rather educators' work is connected to the surrounding community of the school and the external society at large" (Beachum, 2011, p. 33). Singleton and Linton (2006) agreed, stating that educators should make sure that "the administration leads the effort to reach out to all parents and members of the community" (p. 227). In addition, the diversity-conscious school is a place in which

> parents and other community members do not feel disfranchised nor do they feel intimidated due to their own personal educational attainment, English language skills, racial description, economic status, dress, or perceptions of school derived from their own personal experiences. Families know that their voice matters in school affairs. (p. 227)

Reflexive practice overlaps concepts found in Advanced Change Theory and Community Uplift Theory. With regard to ACT, reflexive practice requires the leader to foster new and different kinds of relationships in the organization. "The change agent strives to move self and others from assumptions and strategies of hierarchy to assumptions and strategies of inclusion, openness, and emergent community" (Quinn & Snyder, 1999, pp. 166–167). In addition, leaders personally model integrity, courage, and self-evaluation in an effort to attract others into an environment of "self-exploration, commitment, and growth" (Quinn & Snyder, 1999, p. 169). The final connection with ACT has to do with action. In reflexive practice, like ACT, "there is a trust in emergent processes and a bias toward self-authorizing action. Action experiments are seen as a trial and error process that gives rise to effective learning. Courage and risk taking are central. Failure is an expected part of the learning process" (Quinn & Snyder, 1999, p. 176). This allows the leader to promote different teaching methods, foster innovative collaborative relationships, and take calculated risks in the name of innovation and experimentation. Reflexive practice also adopts the individual and community approach found in CUT. Individually, it encourages school leaders to improve their schools through self-determination and creativity. Self-determination promotes the idea that novel solutions and approaches can come from within and relies on the knowledge, experience, and abilities of the people who work at the school. "Creativity refers to a person's ability to bring an idea/concept into being or from abstraction to fruition" (Beachum et al., 2007, p. 274). In schools, this means finding insightful ways to address some of today's most perplexing educational problems. Examples include peer mediation (student to student); peer evaluations (teacher to teacher); administrators who teach classes' on-site businesses like credit unions' and student-run stores, radio stations, television programs, and websites. Collectively, reflexive practice connects the school with the external community. "Schools can never divorce themselves from the communities where they exist" (Swaminathan, 2005, p. 195). School leaders should foster forums for dialogue and debate, solicit local community members to speak to students, and transform the school into a community hub for events and organizing. When school leaders make meaningful connections with the community, all kinds of excellent programs and endeavors emerge. Examples include on-site school-community liaisons, school-university partnerships (like training grants that fund administrator or teacher preparation), after-school mentoring (McCray et al., 2010), weekend school, and community nights (events that bring the school and surrounding community together). Table 6.1 depicts how Culturally Relevant Leadership intersects ACT, Culturally Relevant Pedagogy, and CUT, as well as its relationship to educational leadership knowledge, disposition, and skills.

Recommendations and Conclusion

The two quotes at the beginning of this chapter highlight the issues of educational inequality and leaders needing to understand context. In this chapter, we presented Culturally Relevant Leadership as a framework to achieve these ends. It addresses educational inequality forcefully by insist-

TABLE 6.1 Culturally Relevant Leadership, Related Theories, and Educational Leadership Qualities

	Advanced Change Theory	Culturally Relevant Pedagogy	Community Uplift Theory	Knowledge	Disposition	Skills
Liberator Consciousness	X	X		X		
Pluralistic Insight		X			X	
Reflexive Practice	X		X			X

ing that educational leaders raise consciousness levels, and this is further undergirded by the personally transformative aspects of ACT and the culture-specific segments of Culturally Relevant Pedagogy. Furthermore, this encourages leaders to not only maintain a critical eye in their schools but also to investigate history and context (such as the history of educational leadership/administration and better understanding the urban context). Pluralistic insight also highlights educational inequity but aligns itself with attitude and disposition. With the number of students of color on the rise and the racial/ethnic homogeneity of the current teaching and leadership force, attitude and disposition toward these students is critical. Moreover, cultural collusion could be at play in situations of cultural misunderstanding or mistrust, so pluralistic insight could help to alleviate such an occurrence. With regard to leadership and context, reflexive practice demands that educational leaders understand their school contexts and surrounding communities. It is guided by the individual/community approach of CUT and driven by the action orientation and strategic vision of ACT. Reflexive practice can also assist the leader in identifying when cultural collision may be taking place and also help with negotiating equitable solutions. Bryant and Jones (1993) described the heart of Culturally Relevant Leadership when they wrote,

> Such administrators break the shackles of the past, moving away from the confines of political conformity. They are visionary and future-oriented. They not only possess images of the high potential to be reached by the teachers and students in their school, but they operate in ways that assure the constant feedback that both motivates and measures organizational change and educational renewal... As leaders they are not tied down either by tradition or the realities of the present. The effective school administrator for today and tomorrow is a change agent. (p. 14)

7

The Intersection of Aestheticism and Administrative Placement at Payton High

(Case Study)

This case is centered on the term "aestheticism," the discrimination or bias against those who do not possess the most desired physical qualities. In this particular case, the authors have chosen to highlight how African American administrators might be selected, assigned, or appointed based on their physical attributes and characteristics. The authors have chosen to reintroduce the term "aestheticism," which originally appeared in Victorian England in the mid-1800s. It had a connotation of an appreciation and dissemination of middle-class beauty with regard to art and style. However, it is the authors' goal in this reintroduction of aestheticism to "ismatize" it as a potential "ism" that highlights a void regarding the covert and overt discrimination that many individuals face on a daily basis as result of physical appearances that are not directly related to their race, ethnicity, religion, or gender.

School Leadership in a Diverse Society, pages 109–122
Copyright © 2014 by Information Age Publishing
109

The short strokes of eyes, nose, mouth, repeated hundreds of times I believe it is which gives the visible law: looked at in any one instance it flies. I could find a short of beauty in this, certainly character—but in fact this is almost synonymous with finding order, anywhere. (Gerard Manley Hopkins, as cited in Fraser, 1986, p. 69)

Fred Jones has been principal of Payton High School for 5 years. He has weathered many different storms related to student and community issues, problems from same-sex dating, and parent rebellions. Through it all, Fred has managed to survive his dream job, which he has held in such high esteem since he walked the halls of Payton High as a student and star athlete. Fred has even managed to solidify many different community factions that have all at some point competed for the few resources Payton High has had at its disposal. One of these groups consisted of parents of color, particularly African Americans, who have complained quietly to Mr. Jones regarding their children being overrepresented in special education classes. Fred is very sensitive to this issue and has done an equity audit in which he has concluded that African American males are disproportionately represented in special education classes as compared with their White counterparts.

Another group Fred has had to contend with was parents who wanted more International Baccalaureate and Advance Placement classes for students in order for Payton High to compete with surrounding schools in the region and to entice additional businesses to relocate to the Payton community. This small but very vocal group has been adamant about the amount of resources, programs, and faculty provided for their children. Many of the parents in this group are not indigenous to the small southern town of Payton. Most of them have upper-level management positions in some of the new companies that have moved into the community and therefore have a significantly higher median income than the local Payton residents. This group is also very diverse in its ethnic, religious, and racial composition. Many of the parents in this group respect Fred as the principal and as an educator. They believe that Fred is trying to do the best for their kids. However, at times the relationship between Fred and this group has been contentious because of Fred's commitment to ensure that all students in his school receive an excellent and equitable education, which in the eyes of many in this group takes away resources from the advanced programs.

Yet another group Fred has identified and worked closely with is the parents who have lived in the community and who have also attended Payton High. This is a group that Fred knows well. He went to school with many of these parents and developed close friendships with nearly all of them.

Many of the parents in this group believe that Fred lost a little of his Payton upbringing when he left the community some 15 years ago to attend college. Many of these parents also cheered for Fred as the quarterback of the Payton High Rebels when he led them to the 3C State Championship. In this southeastern state, schools are classified from 1C to 6C (with 6C being the largest). Payton High has recently grown to be a 5C school with more than 800 students. The sheer increase in size along with the influx of racial, ethnic, and religious diversity is one of the reasons some of the original residents of Payton are grumbling. Many of them see this influx of new residents as an erosion of their influence, a metamorphosis of traditional values, and absolute chaos connected with some of the students of color who have recently come to Payton. The grumbling by the local residents regarding Fred's leadership on these issues is also coupled with their belief that Fred mismanaged the same-sex dating issue at the school prom 5 years earlier. However, most of the local residents have all but forgotten about the same-sex dating issue. But now there is a much different controversy at Payton High School; it is a controversy regarding which African American candidate should be hired for the esteemed assistant principal position.

The Retirement of a Legend

Fred and his search committee have been laboring for weeks with the issue of finding an assistant principal for Payton High. His current assistant principal, Mr. Gene Johnson, decided that he would be calling it quits at the end of the school year. Mr. Johnson had been at Payton High for 35 years, 25 of which were spent as a classroom teacher, while the other 10 were spent as the assistant principal. Fred and Mr. Johnson always had a very good working relationship, and Mr. Johnson was someone whom Fred respected tremendously. But with the retiring of Mr. Johnson, Fred saw an opportunity to bring in a fresh face that would allow him to take Payton High in a different direction, especially with the increasing amount of diversity that was taking place. Mr. Johnson was a legend in the community among the longtime residents. He was known in the community as a no-nonsense type of administrator. Very seldom did he have anyone from the community challenge his authority. Although he was known as a tough disciplinarian, some teachers and parents thought he could not handle the African American males. He was one of those administrators whom the community as well as the faculty and staff were going to hate to see leave. Even though Fred and Mr. Johnson did not necessarily share similar educational philosophies, Fred had tremendous respect for Mr. Johnson.

The Consent Decree

Although there is no denying that most folks in the Payton community would miss Mr. Johnson, many African American parents in the community were beginning to express dissatisfaction with how their children were being treated by him. Many of the parents leveled charges that Mr. Johnson was not giving their students the proper respect and tended to suspend students of color, especially the African American students, at a higher rate than the other students. These parents lobbied for better treatment of their children as well as alternative discipline methods instead of suspension. They were not far off base with their complaints. Even if Mr. Johnson himself was not the direct culprit, documented evidence had been produced by researchers as well as attorneys to support the parents' claims. The Payton County School District had been under a court order for a few years to address some major issues regarding diversity that was evident not only in Payton County but also throughout the state. The court order directed certain counties in the state, including Payton, to address two specific issues. First, many districts were ordered to address the issue of the overrepresentation of African American male students who were being classified as mentally impaired or learning disabled, as well as the issue of the lack of African American students in gifted and talented programs. Second, the courts ordered many districts in the state to make an earnest attempt to hire more racially and ethnically diverse administrators and teachers. Payton High was under both decrees. Out of the nine principals and numerous assistant principals Payton High School has had during its years of existence, all of them have been White males. Faculty of color at Payton High represented 6% of the total number of the teachers, whereas the growing population of African American students had increased from 12% to 16% during the past 5 years. Many African American parents in the Payton community had always been cognizant of these numbers but never felt they had enough cultural and political capital to illuminate the issue. But because of other affluent African American parents moving into the community, along with the court's decree, these issues were now being brought to the forefront.

Finding a New Assistant Principal

Fred Jones knew his school was under the state's decree to hire more people of color and to also reduce the number of African Americans labeled as mentally impaired and learning disabled. He was very sensitive to the issue of diversity. He had come to believe through his extensive travels outside of his home state and via his education that having a diverse faculty and staff was something positive, and it was an area in which he wanted Payton to improve. Although he was sad to see Mr. Johnson leave, he saw it as a wonderful opportunity to bring in potential African American candidates to interview and hire for the assistant principal position. This was something Fred truly wanted, and it was also addressed under the decree. The decree specified that schools must make an earnest effort to have minority candidates as part of the interview process. However, many in the African American community believed that the decree did not go far enough and the earnest effort language was not forceful enough to actually change hiring practices. But Fred knew that the writing was on the wall and felt strongly about bringing more faculty of color into Payton High.

The Cookout

On a Sunday afternoon, Fred met with his Superintendent, Kenneth Wilson, for a cookout and to talk about the assistant principal search. Mr. Wilson, intrigued as to how the search was going, asked, "Fred, how is the search for the new assistant principal coming along?"

Fred responded, "It is coming along well; I think the committee has narrowed down the seven candidates to three; all three of them seem like good choices." Fred indicated to Mr. Wilson that one of Payton's faculty members had made the final cut. "Kenneth, Mike Weber is among the three finalists."

"Well I'll be darned. I didn't know Mike had decided to apply for the position. What are his chances?" asked Mr. Wilson.

"I'm not sure. He's up against some stiff competition. The other two finalists are African American. One is from our neighboring district Rock County, and the other one is from Central City,"

"So we have two Blacks in the pool along with Mike?" asked Mr. Wilson.

"Yes sir!"

"Well, we will have to see how this thing plays out. When is your committee going to come back to you with a recommendation?" Mr. Wilson inquired.

Fred stated, "Well, they are going to interview the final three candidates this week, and they will make their recommendation to me by the end of the week or next Monday. I would like to make a job offer to one of them before the end of the school year."

Wilson then asked, "Fred, does your committee understand that you have a right to go against their recommendation? And remind me again who all is on your committee?"

To this Fred replied, "Well, let's see. We have one African American parent, Ann Sikes; we have Robert Price, the owner of the hardware store; we have Ken Lee, who just recently moved into the community with his family. He has a daughter who is a sophomore. And we have two faculty members, Ms. Harper and Joe Riley. Oh, we also have a student, Chelestie Czant, who is a senior. She is a sharp young lady. She just got an academic and athletic scholarship to the University of Michigan."

"Wow! Well, we are going to hate to see her leave, but maybe she will return to Payton as you did," Mr. Wilson responded.

"Yep, but I think we have a good committee, and they do understand that I have the right to make the final recommendation to you and the board."

"Good deal. Well Fred, who are you pulling for today?" asked Mr. Wilson, as they prepared to watch the Coca Cola 600.

"Kenneth, You know I am a Gordon man!"

Mr. Wilson stated, "Well, you know I am pulling for him too, but he is going to have to make a good showing today because it's a tight race in the point standings. You ready for that beer?"

The Selection Committee

That following Monday morning, Fred's committee started the interview process with the three finalists. The first candidate was Mike Weber, a history teacher at Payton High who recently received his administrative licensure. Mike had been teaching at Payton for 4 years and was recently appointed as one of the assistant football coaches. Mike, who was about 6 ft. 1 in. tall, had been a defensive end on his high school football team. He was the only Caucasian being interviewed. The second candidate was an African American by the name of Chris Thomas, a resident of the adjacent Rock County. Chris was known by some of the residents of Payton for his legendary role as a star basketball player at Rockville High. He went on to play college ball and returned to his community to teach. Chris had a very imposing stature. He stood at 6 ft. 2 in. tall and had a very dark chocolate skin tone. The third candidate was Robert Simms, who had taught math for 9 years and was a rather well-built 5 ft. 6 in. light-skinned African American from Central City. Robert was somewhat of a mystery candidate.

On Monday morning, Fred greeted the committee. "Good morning ladies and gentlemen. I want to take this time to tell you how pleased I am at all of the hard work you have done thus far in helping to find us a new assistant principal. I would like for you to find the best person for the job. As you know, we are under the state's decree to find more minority teachers and administrators. This is a good thing, and this is something I welcome. However, do not feel obligated to send forward someone's name if you feel he is not truly the best person for the job. You know that we need someone who can help provide instructional leadership as well as handle the growing discipline issues. I would like to have this process completed by the end of the week and submit a name to the superintendent and school board ASAP. Also, I want to reiterate that I do have the final decision on the name that will be submitted to the board. But I will take your recommendation with great consideration. And once again, I would like to thank you for your time and energy."

With these instructions, the committee proceeded to interview Mr. Weber that Monday morning. The committee was very impressed with the first candidate. A few of the committee members were pulling for Mr. Weber to get the position. Those committee members who were pulling for him, Robert Price and Ms. Harper, believed that Payton should not hire an outsider, and they had very discerning views in reference to being seemingly forced to hire a minority candidate. But the other committee members had some concerns about Mr. Weber. A few of them believed that he did not have enough experience; others felt that it was time for Payton to make the leap and hire its first minority administrator, if he was qualified. During the discussion following the interview, one of the committee members, Chelestie, questioned Mr. Weber's instructional skills as a classroom teacher. Chelestie, feeling compelled to speak, asked, "May I add something?"

"Sure Chelestie," Mr. Riley responded.

"Well, I know one of the instructions that Mr. Jones gave to us was to find someone we thought would be a good instructional leader. I have had Mr. Weber as a teacher, and I don't think he fits that description."

Ms. Harper quickly interrupted, "Chelestie, I think we should just write down our comments on the evaluation form!"

But Ms. Sikes interjected, "This is the time in which we can voice our concerns about the candidates. And Chelestie is part of this committee. And baby, I've been hearing the same comments from some of the other students and teachers."

At this point, Ms. Harper looked at Mr. Price with a distressful look on her face and then added, "I just don't think a student should be talking about a teacher."

"What does she care? She will be going to Michigan in a few short months," Ms. Sikes added.

The following day (Tuesday), the committee interviewed Chris Thomas.

"Uh, good morning Mr. Thomas," the committee members stated almost in unison as his large frame appeared in the doorway. "Mr. Thomas, please tell us what is the one best qualification you believe you bring to this position," asked Mr. Lee.

Well, let's see, I used to be a star athlete in the neighboring district, Rockville. I left there to attend college and play ball. And of course I returned to teach literature 7 years ago because I thought that I could make a difference. Throughout my 8 years of teaching, I have learned that students need strong discipline. And this is what I have focused on . . . I am a no-nonsense person, and I demand respect from the students, and they are going to give me and my faculty respect. I guess this is the one qualification that I am most proud of thus far."

Mr. Lee, along with Mr. Riley and Chelestie, sat at the table with puzzled looks on their faces, hoping to hear a statement about some instructional methods or leadership styles, while Ms. Harper, Mr. Price, and Ms. Sikes seemed pleased with Mr. Thomas' response. The latter three strongly believed that whoever replaced Mr. Johnson needed to be a strong disciplinarian who could deal with the increasing amount of diversity. And by the latter group's own admission, the young African American males needed an authority figure in the school. Even though Mr. Thomas had demonstrated competence in instructional leadership and other areas, it seems he had been instructed by the administrators at Rockville High to focus heavily on discipline.

On Wednesday morning, the committee was set to interview their final candidate and make their recommendation to Fred the next day after their deliberations. Their final candidate was Robert Simms out of Central City. Robert's principal had seen Payton's posting and had encouraged him to apply. The committee members were extremely impressed with the letter of recommendation his principal wrote for him. In the letter, Simms' principal expressed how dedicated Robert was as a teacher and how he had great potential to be a good instructional leader and an asset to any school system. The letter emphasized Simms' rapport with the students and how much all the students respected him as a teacher and disciplinarian. Some of the committee members felt they had found their assistant principal. It was Robert's job to lose.

Mr. Lee, the chair of the committee, once again led off with the first question. "Mr. Simms, what do you see as your role with regard to being an assistant principal at Payton High?"

"Well, I see my role first and foremost as being an instructional leader for the faculty and helping assist them with pedagogical needs. One of my greatest strengths is my instructional background. I am proud to say that I have my National Board Certification. So I think this is one of the greatest assets I bring to the table."

"Well, Mr. Simms, this is all fine and good, your credentials are impressive, but what about discipline," asked Ms. Harper. She went on to say, "We are having some major issues with student discipline in our school as a result of some of the changing demographics in our community. What is your philosophy on student discipline?"

Mr. Simms took a deep breath and a few seconds to pause and then responded to Ms. Harper's question: "I'm aware of the consent decree. I believe we have to decrease the number of students who are being expelled and suspended first and foremost. Thus, I see that my role will be to work with the faculty to help them understand the potential cultural collision that is happening not only in your school but many other schools in our state and around the country. I suspect that one of the reasons so many students are being expelled, suspended, and tracked into lower levels is because of the disconnect between the students' culture and the culture of the teachers. So I believe instructional leadership and discipline are closely connected. I would implement programs to assist faculty in moving toward a better understanding of this cultural collision, which is connected with the demographic changes, and hopefully start to decrease the number of students who are being sent to the office."

Then Mr. Lee explained, "Well, Mr. Simms, I appreciate you coming down to visit with us today. I am afraid this is all the time we have. The district will get back in touch with you within the next week one way or the other. We expect to make our recommendation to Mr. Jones by the end of the week."

Committee Deliberations

After the interview with Mr. Simms, the committee immediately started its deliberations. Right away the committee members were split in their views. As a result of the fact that Payton was under a court decree, most of the committee members were finally ready to hire Payton's first African American administrator. Also, most of the committee members, except for Ms. Harper and Mr. Price, thought that Mr. Weber was not ready to become assistant principal of Payton. Thus, the decision was now down to the two African American candidates, Mr. Simms and Mr. Thomas.

The committee was evenly split right from the start, with Mr. Lee, Chelestie, and Mr. Riley in the corner of Mr. Simms and with Mr. Thomas receiving the support of Ms. Harper, Mr. Price, and Ms. Sikes. Finally, Ms. Sikes said, "Well, I am just going to go ahead and state the obvious. I think Mr.

Simms is smart and very knowledgeable. And he is going to make someone a good vice principal. But I don't think he is the man for this position."

"Why," Chelestie asked?

"Because I don't think he is going to be able to control these kids. I think whomever we bring into Payton is going to have to be a strong disciplinarian to keep, especially the Black boys, from getting into trouble and being sent home. And I just don't think Mr. Simms is going to be up to the challenge."

Chelestie replied with a slight "Oh!" At this point, Ms. Harper and Mr. Price added their perspectives. Ms. Harper said, "Well, Ann, I am glad to see we finally agree on something! I just don't think this Simms fellow is going to be a good disciplinarian either. I think he will be run over by these kids. And we would probably be doing him a favor because he would almost certainly end up leaving anyway."

"I also concur with Ms. Harper and Ann. This Simms fellow is smart and very articulate, but I just don't think he is the right fit for Payton. I think Thomas would be a much better fit," Mr. Price added.

At this point, Mr. Lee asked them why they felt Mr. Simms would not make a good disciplinarian. He also asked if they were not impressed with his response regarding how he would go about decreasing the suspension and expulsion rates. Then Ms. Harper stated emphatically, "Ken, I just don't think he has the physical presence to deal with these kids like Mr. Thomas has. I mean, when Mr. Thomas walks into a room . . . I mean, my God . . . you know he is in the room. He is big and, uhh, he looks like he doesn't take any mess off of anyone."

"Exactly," said Ms. Sikes. She went on to say, "Mr. Simms is barely bigger than some of the little ninth graders walking around." At this point Ms. Sikes and Ms. Harper both lightly touched each other on the shoulders as they slightly giggled.

"But don't we want someone who is going to be a good instructional leader for the faculty as well as someone who can discipline students?" asked Chelestie. She also pointed out that Mr. Simms had more years of experience than Mr. Thomas and seemed to be the better candidate."

"I agree with Chelestie on this one," said Mr. Riley. "Just because you can tell when Chris comes into a room does not mean he is going to be a better disciplinarian than someone else. If these kids, Black or White, do not respect you and you do not respect them, it is going to be hard for any discipline to take place. And it seems that Mr. Simms has the pulse of students and is also a darn good instructional leader, which is what Fred said he was looking for in a candidate."

Despite both sides going back and forth for their candidate of choice, they could not come to a consensus. Ms. Harper, Ms. Sikes, and Mr. Price were convinced that Mr. Simms was not the person for the job because of his physical presence. They felt that the larger and darker Chris Thomas was indeed the best person, who could keep the students in line, especially the young Black males. On the other side, Mr. Lee, Mr. Riley, and Chelestie were convinced that Mr. Simms had the better résumé and credentials and could be a good instructional leader as well as a disciplinarian. Unfortunately, the committee could not agree on a candidate. Thus, they sent the names of Thomas and Simms to Fred for consideration.

Conclusion

Fred Jones, the principal of Payton High, is now charged with making a decision that cuts through personnel, diversity, instructional, and community relations issues. This is an issue that is new to Fred. Throughout his tenure at Payton High, he has had to deal with many challenges as they relate to diversity. But this is Fred's first instance of dealing with the issue of overt aestheticism—the knowingly discrimination of someone as a result of their physical appearance. In Fred's tenure at Payton High, he has denied many people opportunities to work at Payton because of pseudocultural appearances. He has denied potential employees a position based on their lack of professional attire, weird body piercing, and various hairstyles (e.g., punk, etc.) that he had not considered culturally significant. But Fred knew when he got one of the recommendations back from the committee and the reasoning for preferring Chris Thomas, it was time to take a step back and pause for a minute.

Fred was now faced with the dilemma of potentially denying a person a job based on his natural God-given physical appearance, even though he and three other committee members believed that Mr. Simms was probably the most qualified person for the job. Off the record, the sole reason the three committee members—Ms. Harper, Mr. Price, and Ms. Sikes—gave to Fred for denying Mr. Simms the position was that they did not think he had the physical stature and presence to be a good disciplinarian. Fred wanted his assistant principal to be someone who was a good instructional leader, disciplinarian, and a model for faculty and student behavior. Even though African American males make up only a small portion of the student population at Payton High, Fred took a serious interest in them. He wanted to see his African American males succeed socially and academically. Fred was a White southern male, who found himself committed to the issues of social justice. He questioned the idea of hiring an African American assistant principal simply because he had the desired physical qualities for keeping a certain population in line.

At this point, Fred started to question his own assumptions and beliefs about African American administrators. Could an African American male with Chris's stature and description be what he needed with regard to discipline? Fred also began to reflect back on an article he recently had read that talked about the adversarial role African American administrators have with young Black males. Fred was now wondering whether this could be one of the reasons why such tension might exist between the two. As Fred thought more about the committee's split decision, he continued to have a similar conflict of his own predispositions.

> *It was a hard thing to undo this knot.*
> *The rainbow shines, but only in the thought*
> *Of him that looks. Yet not in that alone,*
> *For who makes rainbows by invention?*
> *And many standing round the waterfall*
> *See one bow each, yet not the same to all,*
> *But each a hand's breadth further than the next.*
> *The sun on falling waters writes the text.*
> *Which is in the eye or the thought.*
> *It was a hard thing to undo this knot.*
> Gerard Manley Hopkins (as cited in Fraser, 1986, p. 79)

Teaching Notes

Finding the right person to fill administrative positions in schools is of vital importance. Care must be taken in the effort to hire the right person, following good management procedures, as well as following all applicable laws. As you answer the following questions, take the above issues into consideration. As background, please familiarize yourself with the following: Title VII of the Civil Rights Act of 1964; the Rehabilitation Act of 1973, Section 504; an article by Gerald Panaro (2003), entitled, "Is Hiring on the Basis of Appearance Illegal?" and an article by Dave Jackson (2007), entitled, "Appearance Discrimination."

Personnel Issues

1. Ms. Sikes was concerned about Mr. Simms' stature. She said he was barely bigger than some of the students. If you were one of the

committee members, would you want to ask Mr. Simms anything about his height and your concern for strong discipline? Why or why not? Can you ask Simms about his height and your concerns about discipline without violating any antidiscrimination laws?

2. Assume that you are Mr. Simms, and the principal did not recommend you for the position. Also assume that you heard from one of Chelestie's parents that the sole reason three of the committee members did not recommend you was due to your stature. Would you have the basis for a lawsuit against the district? What options do you have other than considering a lawsuit?

3. Assume that you are Mr. Simms and that you have been hired. If Ms. Harper has been successful in creating a considerable amount of doubt in your ability to handle the disciplining of African American males, what steps would you take to convince faculty members that you can successfully handle the discipline portion of your job?

4. Should Mr. Jones have reminded the committee of the state's decree to find more minority teachers and administrators? Why or why not? What options, if any, would Mike Weber, the only White candidate, have if he is not hired, given the decree reminder made by Principal Jones?

5. Given the issue of aestheticism, what thoughts do you think were running through Mr. Jones's mind when he started to question his beliefs and assumptions about the role of African American males in education? What theoretical basis do you think Jones had for those beliefs and assumptions?

6. Ms. Sikes, Ms. Harper, and Mr. Price did not want Mr. Simms as assistant principal because of his stature. Does aesthetics sometime have a legitimate role in the hiring of school personnel? Why or why not?

Diversity Issues

1. In the above case, there are two quotations by Gerard Manley Hopkins, a philosopher of aesthetics. What message do you believe is in each of the quotations? How can decision makers utilize these messages in their hiring practices?

2. Is the fact that Payton High has only 6% faculty of color with a 16% student population of color problematic? Why or why not? Also, is the consent decree the best way to address diversity-related issues?

3. Other than the physical appearance of Chris Thomas, what are some other possible reasons why the Payton community, especially

the longtime residents, might be more receptive to him as opposed to the other African American candidate, Robert Simms.

4. It is almost certain that the African American males are not the only ones at Payton High who are misbehaving, yet so much attention has been placed on the need to curtail their bad behavior. Might the aesthetics of the new assistant principal be a major issue if the percentage of minority students was considerably lower? Do you believe this was at the center of Fred questioning his own assumptions and beliefs in the conclusion of the case?

5. Here the authors have chosen to focus on the role aesthetics could possibly play in hiring practices. In what other ways might the issue of aestheticism affect your disposition as a current or future school administrator?

Community Relations Issues

1. Under what conditions is it more beneficial to hire a disciplinarian like Chris Thomas, who emphasizes structure and rules, or an instructional leader like Robert Simms, who focuses on pedagogy and curriculum?

2. In this case, the committee could make only a recommendation to Fred Jones. As a leader, under what circumstances should you disagree with a committee's recommendation? To what extent would Fred's disagreeing with the committee's hiring recommendation undermine his authority and respect among the staff and in the community?

3. Payton High is a school that is well integrated into the local community. If Mike Weber were hired, how could Fred respond to the local African American community?

4. What would you do if you were Fred Jones? How would you release this decision to internal and external publics? What would you do if Kenneth Wilson, the superintendent, disagreed with your decision?

5. Create an agenda for a meeting with the local community to announce the final decision. Who would you invite to speak and why? How would you further support/defend the final decision?

This chapter was reprinted from McCray, C. R., Beachum, F. D., & Richardson, H. (2008). The intersection of aestheticism and administrative placement. *Journal of Cases in Educational Leadership, 11*(1), 44–56.

Leadership for Diversity

Festus E. Obiakor
City University of New York

In social, cultural, economic, political, and educational circles, there appears to be some craving for new and innovative leadership that values diverse voices. In many parts of the world, traditional leaders are experiencing the wrath of the general populace because they are perceived to lack the leadership that appreciates the diversity of their people. Similar problems have intensely manifested themselves from pre-kindergarten to university levels in the United States of America. For example, in many educational circles, we consistently see the victimization and silencing of "outside the box" culturally and linguistically diverse (CLD) voices. The *modus vivendi* has been to play games, work smart (not hard), join the herd mentality, be seen and not be heard. In addition, we see visible circles of leadership failure and mediocrity that are devoid of measurable checks and balances on issues related to diversity. One is forced to ask, Who actually runs the show? It is in this spirit that we must appreciate McCray and Beachum's book, *Leadership in a Diverse Society: Helping Schools Prepare All Students for Success*. It is a book for this day and age!

School Leadership in a Diverse Society, pages 123–126
Copyright © 2014 by Information Age Publishing
123

In this book, McCray and Beachum acknowledge that "this moment in the American educational experience is rife with complexities and ironies." Intriguingly, life sometimes imitates art and vice versa. It is frequently unreal to see the problems that CLD persons confront in education and society; and there appears to be leadership vacuums at almost all levels. Yes, there are no easy answers; yet, leadership continues to matter. A few leadership lessons can be learned from William Shakespeare (Walter J. Black, Inc., 1944) whose phenomenal literary judgments foreshadowed many of today's critical leadership problems. For instance, in his play, *Macbeth*, Duncan was portrayed as a leader who trusted and relied on his followers for both personal and national protection. Duncan was also a passive and weak leader who relied much on a few trusted voices—he never wanted to take charge. Macbeth, one of his able and trusted soldiers, betrayed and killed him even as he bestowed upon him more honors. However, killing Duncan did not bring peace to Macbeth and his dubious wife. Like many of today's leaders, Macbeth wanted to be a king by any means necessary; however, his success in killing Duncan motivated him to kill more so that he would reign as king for a long time, confirming the predictions of the three weird sisters (witches). In the end, his wife died and he was killed miserably; and in his sorrow, he acknowledged that "Life's like a walking shadow" and that "it's like a tale told by an idiot full of sound and fury, yet signifying nothing." Looking at some of today's traditional leaders and borrowing from William Shakespeare's *Macbeth*, it is important to wonder why these so-called leaders do not care about how posterity will remember them, especially how they addressed the plights of disenfranchised, disadvantaged, and at-risk CLD learners.

In *Leadership in a Diverse Society: Helping Schools Prepare All Students for Success*, McCray and Beachum recount Kouzes and Posner's (2007) leadership characteristics (i.e., honesty, forward-looking (visionary), inspiring, and competent). Readers should value these revelations! Leadership is not about firing or hiring people; it is about having the vision that fosters a collaborative, consultative, and cooperative environment. Obviously, this kind of environment must value diversity and embrace the comprehensive support model (CSM) so as to energize students, families, educational professionals (e.g., teachers and leaders), community members, and government agencies (Obiakor, 2001, 2008). In this book, McCray and Beachum clearly emphasize that good leaders must have clear vision. Interestingly, many years ago, this view was posited by McFarland, Senn, and Childress (1993) in their book, *21st Century Leadership: Dialogue with 100 Top Leaders*. They argued that

A clear vision for an organization unifies and inspires. Employees become self-motivated to be a part of the vision and move in that direction. People laboring under the weight of cumbersome hierarchy and ponderous procedures find their efforts often frustrated and their personal initiative crushed. In contrast, it quickly becomes apparent that people have much more to offer when they are self-driven and produce within the context of a powerful vision. (p. 95)

Apparently, a logical extension is that a good leader must believe in people (Tucker, 1984). In his book, *On Becoming a Leader*, the former President of the University of Cincinnati, Warren Bennis (1989), acknowledged that a good leader must (a) master the context, (b) understand the basics, (c) know himself/herself, (d) know the world, (e) operate on instinct, (f) deploy himself/herself—strike hard and try everything, (g) move through chaos, (h) get people on his/her side and understand that organizations can help or hinder, and (i) forge the future. In consonance, Mr. Tim Solso, the CEO of Cummins, a global power company, recalled three fundamental lessons that he learned from his father: "to treat all people with dignity and respect, to do your best every time, and to be true to yourself and your personal values" (Bolsta, 2008, p. 62). In more ways than one, McCray and Beachum, in this book, conclude that vision must be about working with different people to have a unity of purpose and to achieve a common good.

Though *Leadership in a Diverse Society: Helping Schools Prepare All Students for Success* is a book that challenges school leaders, it is also a book that challenges all educational practitioners and service providers. The current systems of identification, assessment/accountability, categorization/labeling, placement, and instruction, must be consistently revisited, especially as they pertain to CLD learners. We need to hear more CLD voices in the leadership circles. As I indicated elsewhere (Obiakor, 2001, 2008), one-dimensional thinking has never yielded the desired dividends in education and related professions. We need truly good leaders who are open-minded and not those who divide and conquer. In addition, we need leaders who can prepare new leaders and not those who specialize in destroying new voices that they might find heretical. From pre-kindergarten to university levels, we have seen leaders who are always "inside the box." These so-called leaders masquerade their bigotry as they pride themselves on being members of a team, or what I call the "sinking ship." Yet, in reality, they are poisonous, visionless elements who seek to destroy new ideas that disrupt their equilibrium. And when they are threatened, they become even more dangerous. Systems that keep these leaders are equally as dangerous as the leaders they preserve. McCray and Beachum summarize that no paradigm can be shifted in education when such leaders are in charge. This is more the reason why most visionary organizations do not compromise quality and equity. School leaders must endeavor to build sailing ships and not sinking ships. As concluded elsewhere (Obiakor & Algozzine, 2011), the sinking ship drowns its occupants!

Leadership in a Diverse Society: Helping Schools Prepare All Students for Success urges us to value multicultural education. As I noted elsewhere (Obiakor, 2011), "While multicultural education requires painstaking sacrifice, altruism, dedication, and commitment at all educational levels…it can be achieved and it must be achieved" (Obiakor, 2011, p. 4). Through their actions, some leaders have been false prophets of multiculturalism. Many of them

> shamelessly use their ill-gotten power, privilege, and influence to (a) intimidate and patronize CLD faculty; (b) "talibanize" new thinking in general and special education; (c) perpetuate traditional misidentification, misassessment, miscategorization, misplacement, and misinstruction; (d) devalue educational quality and equity; and (e) silence and destroy dissenting voices. (Obiakor, 2011, p. 4)

I agree with McCray and Beachum that good leaders must foster realistic multicultural education. Again, as indicated elsewhere (Obiakor & Algozzine, 2011), school leaders and professionals must infuse the kind of education that "creates opportunities, opens doors, expands villages, reduces tribalizations, builds bridges, eliminates racism, engenders trusts, improves collaborative consultations, and grows our future generation" (Obiakor & Algozzine, 2011, p. 4). To a large measure, McCray and Beachum, in this book, have tried to answer our aching multicultural questions.

This book is readable and maintains scholarly clarity. McCray and Beachum use current and pertinent references to buttress their points. I am more than convinced that this book will be a useful tool for school leaders, educators, service providers, and professionals who want to make a measurable difference in the lives of others. It will also be a useful volume for undergraduate and graduate students in teacher education programs, researchers, scholars, and practitioners. In the conclusive words of McCray and Beachum, "We can only hope that this book will have a global impact, but more realistically, we simply hope that it can make your school a better place." Finally, my own hunch is that having this book on your reading list will make you a better person, which will in turn, make our diverse world a better place.

References

Alexander, M. (2010). *The new Jim Crow: Mass incarceration in the age of colorblindness.* New York: The New Press.

Allen, W., & Solorzano, D. (2001). Affirmative action, educational equity, and campus racial climate: A case study of the University of Michigan Law School. *Berkeley La Raza Law Journal, 12,* 237–363.

Allport, G. W. (1954). *The nature of prejudice.* Reading, MA: Addison-Wesley.

Alva, S. (1991). Academic invulnerability among Mexican American students: The importance of protective resources and appraisal. *Hispanic Journal of Behavioral Sciences, 13,* 18–34.

Applebaum, B. (2010). *Being White, being good: White complicity, White moral responsibility, and social justice pedagogy.* Lanham, MD: Rowman & Littlefield.

Au, K., & Kawakami, A. (1994). Cultural congruence in instruction. In E. Hollins, J. King, & W. Hayman (Eds.), *Teaching diverse populations: Formulating knowledge base* (pp. 5–23). Albany: State University of New York Press.

Badaracco, J. (2002). *Leading quietly: An unorthodox guide to doing the right thing.* Harvard Business Press.

Banks, J. A. (1991). Curriculum for empowerment, action, change. In C. Sleeter (Ed.), *Empowerment through multicultural education* (pp. 125–141). New York: State University of New York Press.

Banks, J. A. (1995). Multicultural education: Development, dimensions, and challenges. In J. Joll (Ed.), *Taking sides: Clashing views on controversial education issues* (pp. 84–93). New York, NY: Dushkin.

Banks, J. A. (1996). The African American roots of multicultural education. In J. A Banks (Ed.), *Multicultural education transformative knowledge & action:*

School Leadership in a Diverse Society, pages 127–139
Copyright © 2014 by Information Age Publishing

Historical and contemporary perspectives (pp. 30–45). New York, NY: Teachers College Press.

Banks, J. A. (2001). Multicultural education: Characteristics and goals. In J. A. Banks & C. H. McGee-Banks (Eds.), *Multicultural education: Issues and perspectives* (4th ed., pp. 3–30). New York, NY: John Wiley & Sons.

Banks, J. A., & Banks, C. A. M. (Eds.). (1989). *Multicultural education: Issues and perspectives.* Boston, MA: Allyn & Bacon.

Banks, J. A., & Banks, C. A. M. (Eds.). (1995). *Handbook of research on multicultural education.* New York, NY: Macmillan.

Banks, R. R. (2011). *Is marriage for White people: How the African American marriage decline affects everyone.* New York, NY: Penguin.

Barta, J. (1996). Involving parents in creating an anti-bias class. *Children Today, 18,* 28–33.

Beachum, F. D. (2011). Culturally relevant leadership for complex 21st century school contexts. In F. W. English (Ed.), *Sage encyclopedia of educational leadership and administration* (2nd ed.). Thousand Oaks, CA: Sage.

Beachum, F. D., & Dentith, A. M. (2004). Teacher leaders: Creating cultures of school renewal and transformation. *Educational Forum, 68*(3), 276–286.

Beachum, F. D., & McCray, C. R. (2004). Cultural collision in urban schools. *Current Issues in Education, 7*(5). Retrieved from http://cie.asu.edu/volume7/number5/

Beachum, F. D., & McCray, C. R. (2008a). Dealing with cultural collision: What pre-service teachers should know. In G. S. Goodman (Eds.), *Educational psychology: An application of critical constructivism.* New York, NY: Peter Lang.

Beachum, F. D., & McCray, C. R. (2008b). Leadership in the eye of the storm: Challenges at the intersection of urban schools, cultural collusion, and *No Child Left Behind. Multicultural Learning and Teaching, 3*(2). Retrieved from http://www.mltonline.org/current-articles/mlt-3-2/beachum-mccray.pdf

Beachum, F. D., & McCray, C. R. (2011). *Cultural collision and collusion: Reflections on hip-hop culture, values, and schools.* New York, NY: Peter Lang.

Beachum, F. D., & McCray, C. R. (2012). The fast and the serious: Exploring the notion of culturally relevant leadership. In J. Moore & C. W. Lewis (Eds.), *Urban school contexts for African American students: Crisis and prospects for improvement* (pp. 231–247). New York, NY: Peter Lang.

Beachum, F. D., McCray, C. M., & Huang, T. (2010). Administrators and teachers sharing leadership: Utilizing C.A.R.E. in urban schools. *Making Connections, 12*(1), 51–62.

Beachum, F. D., & Obiakor, F. E. (2005). Educational leadership in urban schools. In F. E. Obiakor & F. D. Beachum (Eds.), *Urban education for the 21st century: Research, issues, and perspectives* (pp. 83–99). Springfield, IL: Charles C. Thomas

Beachum, F. D., Obiakor, F. E., & McCray, C. R. (2007). Community uplift theory for positive change of African Americans in urban schools. In M. C.

Brown & R. D. Bartee (Eds.), *Still not equal: Expanding educational opportunity in society* (pp. 269–278). New York, NY: Peter Lang.

Bennis W. (1989). *On becoming a leader.* Reading, MA: Addison-Wesley.

Berliner, D. (2006). Our impoverished view of educational research. *Teachers College Record, 108,* 949–955.

Blumenfeld, W. J., & Raymond, D. (2000). Prejudice and discrimination. In M. Adams, W. J. Blumenfeld, R. Castaneda, H. W. Hackman, M. L. Peters, & X. Zuniga (Eds.), *Reading for diversity and social justice: An anthology on racism, anti-Semitism, sexism, heterosexism, ableism, and classism* (pp. 21–30). New York, NY: Routledge.

Bogotch, I. (2002). Educational leadership and social justice: Practice into theory. *Journal of School Leadership, 12*(2), 138–156.

Bogotch, I. (2011). A history of public school leadership: The first century 1837–1942. In F. English (Ed.), The Sage handbook of educational leadership: Advances in theory,research, and practice. Thousand Oaks, CA: Sage.

Bogotch, I., Beachum, F. D., Blount, J., Brooks, J., & English, F. W. (2008). *Radicalizing educational leadership: Dimensions of social justice.* Rotterdam, The Netherlands: Sense.

Bolsta, P. (2008, May). Executive interview: Tim Solso. *WorldTraveler,* p. 64.

Boske, C. (2012). Educational leadership: Building bridges among ideas, schools, and nations. Charlotte, NC: Information Age.

Bourdieu, P., & Passeron, J. C. (1977). *Reproduction in education, society, and culture.* London, UK: Sage.

Bowles, S., & Gintis, H. (1976). *Schooling in capitalist America: Educational reform and the contradiction of economic life.* New York, NY: Basic.

Brown, F. (2005). African Americans and school leadership: An introduction. *Educational Administration Quarterly, 41*(4), 585–590.

Bryant, B., & Jones, A. H. (1993). *Seeking effective schools for African American children.* San Francisco, CA: Caddo Gap.

Calculator, C. I. (2010). *Bureau of Labor Statistics.* Washington, DC, USA http://www. bls. gov/cpi.

Callahan, R. E. (1962). *Education and the cult of efficiency.* Chicago, IL: University of Chicago Press.

Calms, J. (2011, March 10). Obama's focus on antibullying efforts. *New York Times.* Retrieved from http://www.nytimes.com

Cosby, B., & Poissaint, A. F. (2007). *Come on people: On the path from victims to victors.* Nashville, TN: Thomas Nelson.

Council of the Great City Schools. (2010). *A call for change: The social and educational factors contributing to the outcomes of Black males in urban schools.* Washington, DC.

Cox, T., Jr. (1994). *Cultural diversity in organizations: Theory, research, and practice.* San Francisco, CA: Berrett-Koehler.

Cox, T., Jr. (2001). *Creating the multicultural organization: A strategy for capturing the power of diversity.* San Francisco, CA: Jossey-Bass.

Cremin, L. A. (1961). The transformation of the school: *Progressivism in American education, 1876–1957 (Vol. 519).* New York: Knopf.

Cuban, L. (2004). Looking through the rearview mirror at school accountability. In K. A. Sirotnik (Ed.), *Holding accountability accountable: What ought to matter in public education.* New York, NY: Teachers College Press.

Cunningham, W. G., & Cordeiro, P. A. (2003). *Educational leadership: A problem-based approach* (2nd ed.). Boston, MA: Allyn and Bacon.

Dantley, M. E. (2002). Uprooting and replacing positivism, the melting pot, multiculturalism, and other impotent notions in educational leadership through an African American perspective. *Education and Urban Society, 34*(3), 334–352.

Dantley, M. E. (2005). African American spirituality and Cornel West's notions of prophetic pragmatism: Restructuring educational leadership in American urban schools. *Educational Administration Quarterly, 41*(4), 651–674.

Dantley, M. E. (2009). African American educational leadership: Critical, purposive, and spiritual. In L. F. Foster & L. C. Tillman (Eds.), *African American perspectives on leadership in schools: Building a culture of empowerment.* Lanham, MD: Rowman & Littlefield Education.

Dantley, M. E. (2010). Successful leadership in urban schools: Principals and critical spirituality: A new approach to reform. *The Journal of Negro Education, 79*(3), 214–219.

Dantley, M. E., Beachum, F. D., & McCray, C. R. (2008). Exploring the intersectionality of multiple centers within notions of social justice. *Journal of School Leadership, 18*(2), 124–133.

Dantley, M. E., & Tillman, L. C. (2010). Social justice and moral transformative leadership. In C. Marshall & M. Oliva (Eds.), *Leadership for social justice.* New York, NY: Allyn & Bacon.

Darling-Hammond, L. (1995). Inequality and access to knowledge. In J. Banks (Ed.), *Handbook of multicultural education* (pp. 465–483). New York, NY: Macmillan.

Day-Vines, N. L., & Day-Hairston, B. O. (2005). Culturally congruent strategies for addressing the behavioral needs of urban, African American male adolescents. *Professional School Counseling, 8*(1), 236–243.

DeCuir, J. T., & Dixson, A. D. (2004). "So when it comes out, they aren't that surprised that it is there": Using critical race theory as a tool of analysis of race and racism in education. *Educational Researcher, 33*(5), 26–31.

Diaz-Lazaro, C., & Cohen, B. B. (2001). Cross-cultural contact in counseling training. *Journal of multicultural counseling and development, 29*(1), 41–56

Dyson, M. E. (2004). *The Michael Eric Dyson reader.* New York, NY: Basic Civitas.

Dyson, M. E. (2009). *Can you hear me now?: The inspiration, wisdom, and insight of Michael Eric Dyson.* New York, NY: Basic Civitas.

English, F. W. (2008). *The art of educational leadership: Balancing performance and accountability.* Thousand Oaks, CA: Sage.

Epps, E. G. (2005). Urban education: Future perspectives. In F. E. Obiakor & F. D. Beachum (Eds.), *Urban education for the 21st century: Research, issues, and perspectives* (pp. 218–234). Springfield, IL: Charles C. Thomas.

Feagin, J. R., & Feagin, C. B. (1978). *Discrimination American style: Instructional racism and sexism.* Malabar, FL: Kreiger.

Ferguson, A. A. (2001). *Bad boys: Public school in the making of Black masculinity.* Ann Arbor, MI: University of Michigan Press.

Ferguson, R. M. (2008). *Toward Excellence with Equity: An Emerging Vision for Closing the Achievement Gap.* Cambridge, MA: Harvard Education Press.

Foster, L. (2009). Leadership in K–12 schools for promoting educational aspirations: A mental model for school advancement. In L. Foster & L. C. Tillman (Eds.), *African American perspectives on leadership in schools. Building a culture of empowerment* (pp. 157–170). Lanham, MD: Rowman & Littlefield Education.

Fraser, H. (1986). *Beauty and belief: Aesthetics and religion in Victorian literature.* London, UK: Cambridge University Press.

Freire, P. (1970). *Pedagogy of the oppressed.* New York, NY: Seabury.

Freire, P. (1998). *Pedagogy of Freedom: Ethics, democracy, and civic courage.* Lanham, Maryland: Rowman & Littlefield Publishers, INC.

Friedland, R. (1983). *Power and crisis in the city.* New York, NY: Schocken.

Friedman, T. L. (2005). *The world is flat: A brief history of the twenty-first century.* New York, NY: Farrar, Straus and Giroux.

Fullan, M. (2004). *Leading in a culture of change: Personal action guide and workbook.* San Francisco, CA: Jossey-Bass.

Gay, G. (1995, Fall). Building multicultural theory and practice. *Multicultural Education, 54–58.*

Gewirtz, S. (1998). Conceptualizing social justice in education: Mapping the territory. *Journal of Educational Policy, 13*(4), 469–484.

Gordon, M. M. (1978). *Human nature, class, and ethnicity.* New York, NY: Oxford University Press.

Gorski, P. (2006). The unintentional undermining of multicultural education: Educators at the crossroads. In J. L. Landsman & C. W. Lewis (Eds.), *White teachers/diverse classrooms: A guide to building inclusive schools, promoting high expectations, and eliminating racism* (pp. 61–78). Sterling, VA: Stylus.

Gould, S. J. (1996). *The mismeasure of man.* New York, NY: W.W. Norton.

Grant, C. A. (1995, Summer). Reflections on the promise of *Brown* and multicultural education. *Teachers College Record, 707–721.*

Haberman, M. (2005). Personnel preparation and urban schools. In F. E. Obiakor & F. D. Beachum (Eds.), *Urban education for the 21st century: Research issues and perspectives.* Springfield, IL: Charles C. Thomas.

Halperin, S. (2008). *The forgotten half revisited: American youth and young families, 1988–2008.* Washington, DC: American Youth Policy Forum.

Hancock, S. D. (2006). White women's work: On the front lines of urban education. In J. Landsman & C. W. Lewis (Eds.), *White teachers/diverse classrooms:*

A guide to building inclusive schools, promoting high expectations, and eliminating racism (pp. 93–109). Sterling, VA: Stylus.

Hardiman, R., & Jackson, B. W. (1997). Conceptual foundation for social justice courses. In M. Adams, L. A. Bell, & P. Griffin (Eds.), *Teaching for diversity and social justice: A sourcebook*. New York, NY: Routledge.

Harris, A. L. (2011). *Kids don't want to fail: Oppositional culture and the Black-White achievement gap*. Cambridge, MA: Harvard University Press.

Harro, B. (2000). The cycle of socialization. In M. Adams, W. J. Blumenfield, R. Castaneda, H. W. Hackman, M. L. Peters, & X. Zuniga (Eds.), *Reading for diversity and social justice: An anthology on racism, anti-Semitism, sexism, heterosexism, ableism, and classism* (pp. 79–82). New York, NY: Routledge.

Hersey, P., Blanchard, K. H., & Johnson, D. E. (1996). *Management of organizational behavior: Utilizing human resources*. Upper Saddle River, NJ: Prentice Hall.

Hewitt, T. W. (2008). Speculations on a nation at risk: Illusions and realities. *Phi Delta Kappan, 89*(8), 575–579.

Hodgkinson, H. L. (1998). *Predicting demographics in the nation's schools*. Washington, DC: Center for Democratic Policy, Institute for Educational Leadership.

Hostetler, K. (2005). What is "good" educational research? Educational Researcher, 34(6), 16–21.

Houser, N. O. (1996). Multicultural education for the dominant culture: Toward the development of a multicultural sense of self. *Urban Education, 31,* 125–148.

Howard, T. C. (2003). Culturally relevant pedagogy: Ingredients for critical teacher reflection. *Theory into Practice, 42*(3), 195–202.

Irvine, J. J. (1990). *Black students and school failure*. New York, NY: Greenwood.

Irvine, J. J. (2010). Culturally relevant pedagogy. *The Education Digest, 75*(8), 5.

Jackson, D. (2007). *Appearance discrimination*. Retrieved April 25, 2007, from http://www.active.org.au/ perth/news/front.php3?article_id2797&groupwebcast

Jackson, J. H. (2008). *Given half a chance: The Schott 50 state report on public education and African American males*. Cambridge, MA: Schott Foundation for Public Education.

Jerald, C. (2002). *All talk, no action: Putting an end to out of field teaching*. Retrieved December 5, 2006, from http://www2.edtrust.org/NR/rdonlyres/8DE64524-592E-4C83-A13A-6B1DF1CF8D3E/0/AllTalk.pdf

Kailin, J. (2002). *Antiracist education: From theory to practice*. Lanham, MD: Rowman & Littlefield.

Karpinski, C. F., & Lugg, C. A. (2006). Social justice and educational administration: Mutually exclusive? *Journal of Educational Administration, 44*(3), 278–292.

Kaufman, R. (1995). *Mapping educational success: Strategic thinking and planning for school administrators*. Thousand Oaks, CA: Corwin.

Kouzes, J. M., & Posner, B. Z. (2007). *The leadership challenge* (4th ed.). San Francisco, CA: Wiley & Sons.

Kozol, J. (2012). *Savage inequalities: Children in America's schools.* New York, NY: Broadway.

Krugman, P. (2011, November 21). Boring Cruel Romantics. *New York Times,* p. A29.

Kunjufu, J. (2002). *Black students-Middle class teachers.* Chicago, IL: African American Images.

Ladson-Billings, G. (1994). *The dreamkeepers: Successful teachers of African-American students.* San Francisco, CA: Jossey-Bass.

Ladson-Billings, G. (1995). But that's just good teaching! The case for culturally relevant pedagogy. *Theory into Practice, 34,* 159–165.

Larson, C. L., & Ovando, C. J. (2001). *The color of bureaucracy: The politics of equity in multicultural school communities.* Belmont, CA: Wadsworth.

Lee, C. D. (1995). Signifying as a scaffold for literary interpretation. *Journal of Black Psychology, 21,* 357–381.

Lewis, C. W., James, M., Hancock, S., & Hill-Jackson, V. (2008). Framing African American students' success and failure in urban settings: A typology for change. *Urban Education, 43*(2), 127–153.

Lindsey, R. B., Roberts, L. M., & Campbell Jones, F. (2005). *The culturally proficient school: An implementation guide for school leaders.* Thousand Oaks, CA: Corwin.

Lynch, M. (2006). *Closing the racial academic achievement gap.* Chicago, IL: African American Images.

Marriot, D. (2001). Managing school culture. *Principal, 81*(1), 75–77.

Marshall, C., & Olivia, M. (Eds.). (2006). Leadership for social justice: Making revolutions in education. Boston, MA: Pearson Education.

Mayeroff, M. (1971). *On caring.* New York, NY: Harper Perennial.

McCray, C. R. (2008). *Constructing a positive intrasection of race and class for the 21st century. Journal of School Leadership, 18*(2), 249–267.

McCray, C. R. (2010) A holistic and critical analysis of principals' perceptions of multicultural education. *Journal of Non-Significant Results, 1*(1), 37–52.

McCray, C. R., Alston, J. A., & Beachum, F. D. (2006). Principals' perceptions of multicultural education and school climate. *Multicultural Learning and Teaching, 1*(1), 12–22.

McCray, C. R., & Beachum, F. D. (2006). A critique of zero tolerance policies: An issue of justice and caring. *Values and Ethics in Educational Administration, 5*(1), 1–8. Retrieved from http://www.ed.psu.edu/UCEACSLE/VEEA/VEEA_Vol5Num1.pdf

McCray, C. R., & Beachum, F. (2010). An analysis of how the gender and race of school principals influences their perceptions of multicultural education. *International Journal of Education Policy and Leadership, 5*(4). Retrieved from http://www.ijepl.org

McCray, C. R., & Beachum, F. D. (2011a). Culturally relevant leadership for the enhancement of teaching and learning in urban schools. In I. Bogotch (Ed.), *International handbook on leadership for learning* (pp. 487–501). Van Godewijckstraat, The Netherlands: Springer.

McCray, C. R., & Beachum, F. D. (2011b). Capital matters: A pedagogy of self-development: Making room for alternative forms of capital. In R. Bartee (Ed.), *Contemporary perspectives on capital in educational context* (pp. 79–100). Charlotte, NC: Information Age.

McCray, C. R., Beachum, F. D., & Richardson, H. (2008). The intersection of aestheticism and administrative placement. *Journal of Cases in Educational Leadership, 11*(1), 44–56.

McCray, C. R., Grant, C., &., Beachum, F. D. (2010). Pedagogy of self-development: The role the Black church can have on African American students. *Journal of Negro Education, 79*(3), 233–248.

McCray, C. R., Pauken, P., & Beachum, F. D. (2004). Taboo dating in the 21st century at Payton High School. *Journal of Cases in Educational Leadership*. Retrieved from http://www.ucea.org/~ucea/cases/V7-Iss3/pdf/FC-Taboo%20Dating%20FE.pdf

McCray, C. R., Wright, J. V., & Beachum, F. D. (2004). An analysis of secondary school principals' perceptions of multicultural education. *Education, 125*(1), 111–120.

McCray, C. R., Wright, J. V., & Beachum, F. D. (2007). Beyond *Brown*: Examining the perplexing plight of African American principals. *Journal of Instructional Psychology, 34*(4), 247–255.

McFarland, L. J., Senn, L. E., & Childress, J. R. (1993). *21st century leadership: Dialogues with 100 top leaders.* New York, NY: Leadership.

McKinsey & Company. (2009). The economic impact of the achievement gap in America's schools. *The McKinsey & Company Social Sector Office.* Retrieved from http://www.mckinsey.com/app_media/images/page_images/offices/socialsector/pdf/achievement_gap_report.pdf

McLaren, P. (1997). *Revolutionary multiculturalism: Pedagogies of dissent for the new millennium.* Boulder, CO: Westview.

Miller, P. M., Brown, T., & Hopson, R. (2011). Creating love, hope, and trust in the community: Transformative urban leadership informed by Paulo Freire. *Urban Education, 46,* 1078–1099.

Milner, H. R. (2006). But good intentions are not enough: Theoretical and philosophical relevance in teaching students of color. In J. Landsman & C. W. Lewis (Eds.), *White teachers/diverse classrooms: A guide to building inclusive schools, promoting high expectations, and eliminating racism* (pp. 79–90). Sterling, VA: Stylus.

Milner, H. R. (2010). *Start where you are but don't stay there: Understanding diversity, opportunity gaps, and teaching in today's classrooms.* Cambridge, MA: Harvard Education Press.

Mizialko, A. (2005). Reducing the power of "Whiteness" in urban schools. In F. E. Obiakor & F. D. Beachum (Eds.), *Urban education for the 21st century:*

Research, issues, and perspectives (pp. 176–186). Springfield, IL: Charles C. Thomas.

Morris, J. E. (2009). *Troubling the waters: Fulfilling the promise of quality public schooling for Black children.* New York, NY: Teachers College Press.

National Center for Education Statistics (NCES). (1998). *Data file:1996–97 common core of data public elementary and secondary school universe.* Washington, DC: U.S. Government Printing Office.

New York Times. (2010a, December 1). *A mission to transform Baltimore beaten schools.*

New York Times. (2010b, December 7). *Top test scores from Shanghai stun educators.*

Nieto, S. (2000). *Affirming diversity: The sociopolitical context of multicultural.* New York, NY: Longman.

Nieto, S., & Bode, P. (2008). *Affirming diversity: The sociopolitical context of multicultural education* (5th ed.). Boston, MA: Allyn and Bacon.

Nisbett, R. E. (2009). *Intelligence and how to get it. Why schools and cultures count.* New York, NY: Norton.

Noguera, P. A. (2008). *The trouble with Black boys: . . . And other reflections on race, equity, and the future of public education.* San Francisco, CA: Jossey Bass.

Obiakor, F. E. (2001). *It even happens in "good" schools: Responding to cultural diversity in today's classrooms.* Thousand Oaks, CA: Corwin.

Obiakor, F. E. (2008). *The eight-step approach to multicultural learning and teaching* (3rd ed.). Dubuque, IA: Kendall Hunt.

Obiakor, F. E. (2011). Beware of false prophets of multicultural education. *Multicultural Learning and Teaching, 6*(2), 1–6.

Obiakor, F. E., & Algozzine, B. (2011). Leadership in education and the "vision" thing. *Multicultural Learning and Teaching, 6*(1), 1–4.

Obiakor, F. E., & Beachum, F. D. (2005). Developing self-empowerment in African-American students using the comprehensive support model. *The Journal of Negro Education, 74*(1), 18–29.

Obiakor, F. E., Beachum, F. D., McCray, C. R., Mutua, K., Harris, M. K., & Offor, M. T. (2012). Debunking perceptions to enhance culturally responsive teaching and leadership. *Scholar and Educator, 31*(2011/2012), 7–26.

Obiakor, F. E., & Ford, B. A. (2002). *Creating successful learning environments for African American learners with exceptionalities.* Thousand Oaks, CA: Corwin.

Obiakor, F. E., Harris, M. K., & Beachum, F. D. (2009). The state of special education for African American learners in Milwaukee. In G. L. Williams & F. E. Obiakor (Eds.), *The state of education of urban learners and possible solutions: The Milwaukee experience* (pp. 31–48). Dubuque, IA: Kendall Hunt.

Ortiz, F. I. (1982). Career patterns in education: Women, men, and minorities, in public school administration. South Hadley, MA: J. F. Bergin.

Owens, R. G. (2001). *Organizational behavior in education: Instructional leadership and reform.* Boston, MA: Allyn and Bacon.

Panaro, G. (2003). *Is hiring on the basis of appearance illegal?* Retrieved April 25, 2007, from http://www.bankersonline.com/operations/gp_appearance.html

Payzant, T. (2011). *Urban school leadership.* San Francisco, CA: Jossey-Bass.

Perry, T. (2003). Up from the parched earth: Toward a theory of African-American achievement. In T. Perry, C. Steel, & A. G. Hilliard (Eds.), *Young, gifted and Black: Promoting high achievement among African-American students* (pp. 1–108). Boston, MA: Beacon.

Perry, T., Steele, C., & Hilliard, A. (2003). *Young, gifted and Black: Promoting high achievement among African American students.* Boston, MA: Beacon.

Peterson, R. L. (2003). Teaching the social curriculum: School discipline as instruction. *Preventing School Failure, 47*(2), 66–73.

Pink, D. A. (2006). *A whole new mind: Why right-brainers will rule the future.* New York, NY: Riverhead.

Quinn, R. E., & Snyder, N. T. (1999). Advanced change theory: Culture change at Whirlpool corporation. In J. A. Conger, G. M. Speitzer, & E. E. Lawler III (Eds.), *The leader's change handbook: An essential guide to setting direction & taking action* (pp. 162–194). San Francisco, CA: Jossey-Bass.

Radd, S. I. (2008). Looking for social justice: Competing perspectives as methodological instrument in a study of school leaders for social justice. *Journal of School Leadership, 18*(2), 268–286.

Ramirez, M., & Castaneda, A. (1974) *Cultural democracy, biocognitive development and education.* New York, NY: Academic.

Ravitch, D. (2010). *The death and life of the great American school system: How testing and choice are undermining education.* New York, NY: Basic.

Reed, L. C. (2008). An expansion of a scholar's social justice perspective: A meeting at the crossroads. *Journal of School Leadership, 18*(2), 200–223.

Reid, K. S. (2003). N.Y.C. to expand school for gay, lesbian youth. *Education Week, 22*(43).

Rist, R. (1970). Student social class and teacher expectations: The self-fulfilling prophecy in ghetto education. *Harvard Educational Review, 40*(3), 411–451.

Rosenthal, R., & Jacobson, L. (1969). *Pygmalion in the classroom: Teacher expectations and pupils' intellectual achievement.* New York, NY: Holt, Rinehart and Winston.

Russo, C. J. (2004). One step forward, half a step backward. *The Journal of Negro Education, 73*(3), 174–181.

Ryan, J. (2006). *Inclusive leadership.* San Francisco, CA: Jossey-Bass.

Scheurich, J. J., & Skrla, L. (2003). Leadership for equity and excellence: Creating high- achievement classroom, schools, and districts. Thousand Oaks, CA: Corwin.

Scholte, J. A. (2000). *Globalization: A critical introduction.* New York, NY: St. Martin's.

Schoorman, D., & Bogotch, I. (2010). What is a critical multicultural researcher? A self-reflective study of the role of the researcher. Education, Citizenship and Social Justice, 5(3) 249–264.

Schott Foundation for Public Education. (2010). *Yes we can: The Schott 50 State Report on Public Education and Black males.* Cambridge, MA: Schott Foundation.

Shade, B. J., Kelly, C., & Oberg, M. (1997). *Creating culturally responsive classrooms.* Washington, DC: American Psychological Association.

Shields, C. (2012). Transformative leadership reader. New York, NY: Peter Lang.

Shoho, A. R., Merchant, B. M., & Lugg, C. A. (2005). Social justice: Seeking a common language. In F. W. English (Ed.), *The Sage handbook of educational leadership: Advances in theory, research and practice* (pp. 47–67). Thousand Oaks, CA: Sage.

Singleton, G. E., & Linton, C. (2006). *Courageous conversations about race: A field guide for achieving equity in schools.* Thousand Oakes, CA: Corwin.

Skiba, R. J., & Peterson, R. L. (1999). The dark side of zero tolerance: Can punishment lead to safe schools? *Phi Delta Kappan, 80*(5), 372–376.

Skrla, L., McKenzie, K., & Scheurich, J. (2009). *Using equity audits to create equitable and excellent schools.* Thousand Oaks, CA: Corwin.

Skrla, L., Scheurich, J. J., Garcia, J., & Nolly, G. (2004). Equity audits: A practical leadership tool for developing equitable and excellent schools. *Educational Administration Quarterly, 40*(1), 133–161.

Sleeter, C. E. (1996). *Multicultural education as social activism.* Albany: State University of New York Press.

Sleeter, C. E., & Grant, C. A. (1987). An analysis of multicultural education in the United States. *Harvard Educational Review, 57,* 421–444.

Smith, K. (2011, Jully 22). Anoka-Hennepin sue over bullying. *StarTribune.* Retrieved from http://www.startribune.com/local/north/125958688.html

Solorzano, D. G. (1997). Images and words that wound: Critical race theory, racial stereotyping, and teacher education. *Teacher Education Quarterly, 24*(3), 5–19.

Starratt, R. J. (1991). Building an ethical school: A theory of practice in educational leadership. *Educational Administration Quarterly, 27,* 185–202.

Starratt, R. J. (2004). *Ethical leadership.* San Francisco, CA: Jossey-Bass.

Swaminathan, R. (2005). Building community in urban schools: Promises and challenges. In F. E. Obiakor & F. D. Beachum (Eds.), *Urban education for the 21st century: Research, issues, and perspectives* (pp. 187–197). Springfield, IL: Charles C. Thomas.

Tatum, B. D. (1997). *Why are all the Black kids sitting together in the cafeteria.* New York: Basic Books.

Tatum, B. D. (2007). *Can we talk about race? And other conversations in an era of school resegregation.* Boston, MA: Beacon.

Taylor, E. (2000, June). Critical race theory in the backlash against affirmative action. *Teachers College Record,* 539–560.

Terman, L. M. (1916). *The measurement of intelligence.* Boston, MA: Houghton Mifflin.

Terrell, R. D., & Lindsey, R. B. (2009). *Culturally proficient leadership: The personal journey begins within.* Thousand Oaks, CA: Corwin.

Theoharis, G. (2009). *The school leaders our children deserve: Seven keys to equity, social justice, and school reform.* New York, NY: Teachers College Press.

Tillman, L. C. (2003, Fall). From rhetoric to reality? Educational administration and the lack of racial and ethnic diversity within the profession. *University Council for Educational Review, 14*(3), 1–4.

Tooms, A., & Boske, C. (2010). Building bridges: Connecting educational leadership and social justice to improve schools. Charlotte, NC: Information Age.

Tosh, K. & Edwards, C. J. (2009). *The new Title I: The changing landscape of accountability.* Washington, DC: Thompson.

Tucker, A. (1984). *Chairing the academic department: Leadership among peers* (2nd ed.). New York, NY: American Council on Education.

Tyack, D. (1974). *The one best system: A history of American urban education.* Cambridge, MA: Harvard University Press.

Tyack, D., & Hansot, E. (1982). *Managers of virtue: Public school leadership in America 1829–1980.* New York, NY: Basic.

U.S. Census Bureau. (2000). Retrieved December 14, 2001, from http://www. ew.com/ew/interstitials/inter_2for1

Villegas, A. M., & Lucas, T. (2002a). Preparing culturally responsive teachers: Rethinking the curriculum. *Journal of Teacher Education, 53*(1), 20–32.

Villegas, A. M., & Lucas, T. (2002b). *Educating culturally responsive teachers: A coherent approach.* Albany: State University of New York Press.

Wacquant, L. (2001). Deadly symbiosis: When ghetto and prison meet and mesh. *Punishment and Society, 3*(1), 95–134.

Wagner, T. (2008). *The global achievement gap: Why even our best schools don't teach the new survival skills our children need—and what we can do about it.* New York, NY: Basic.

Walker, V., & Snarey, J. (2004). *Race-ing moral formation: African-American perspectives on care and justice.* Williston, VT: Teachers College Press.

Walter J. Black, Inc. (1944). *The works of William Shakespeare.* Roslyn, NY: Black's Readers Service.

Walters, D. J. (1987). *The art of leadership: A practical guide for people in positions of responsibility.* New York, NY: MJF.

Washington, J. M. (1991). *A testament of hope: The essential writings and speeches of Martin Luther King Jr.* New York, NY: First Harper Collins.

Waters, K. (2011). Teenage bullies: Might not right. *Phi Kappa Forum, 91*(1), 7–9.

West, C. (2004). *Democracy matters: Winning the fight against imperialism.* New York, NY: Penguin.

West, C. (2008). *Hope on a tightrope: Words and wisdom.* Carlsbad, CA: Hay House.

Wilkerson, I. (2010). *The warmth of other suns: The epic story of America's great migration.* New York, NY: Random House.

Wilson, W. J. (2009). *More than just race: Being Black and poor in the inner city.* New York, NY: W. W. Norton.

Wittig, M., & Grant-Thompson, S. (1998). The utility of Allport's conditions of intergroup contact for predicting perceptions of improved racial attitudes and beliefs. *Journal of Social Sciences, 54,* 795–812.

Wright, A. N., & Tolan, J. (2009). Prejudice reduction through shared adventure: A qualitative outcome assessment of a multicultural education class. *Journal of Experiential Education, 32*(2), 137–154.

Yosso, T. J. (2005). Whose culture has capital? A critical race theory discussion of community cultural wealth. *Race, Ethnicity, and Education, 8,* 69–91.

Young, E. L., Nelson, D. A., Hottle, A. B., Warburtonm, B., & Young, B. K. (2011, March). Relational aggression among students. *Principal Leadership, 11,* 12–16.

Zamudio, M. M., Russell, C., Rios, F. A., & Bridgeman, J. L. (2011). *Critical race theory matters: Education and ideology.* New York, NY: Routledge.